THE AUTOBIOGRAPHY OF AN AFRICAN

DANIEL MTUSU

THE AUTOBIOGRAPHY OF AN AFRICAN

RETOLD IN BIOGRAPHICAL FORM & IN THE
WILD AFRICAN SETTING OF THE LIFE OF

DANIEL MTUSU

BY

DONALD FRASER, D.D.

AUTHOR OF
"AFRICAN IDYLLS," "WINNING A PRIMITIVE PEOPLE,"
"THE FUTURE OF AFRICA," &c., &c.

ILLUSTRATED

NEGRO UNIVERSITIES PRESS
WESTPORT, CONNECTICUT

o

Originally published in 1925
by Seeley, Service & Co., Ltd., London

Reprinted in 1970 by Negro Universities Press
A Division of Greenwood Press, Inc.
Westport, Connecticut

Library of Congress Catalogue Card Number 78-138006

SBN 8371-5653-X

Printed in the United States of America

AUTHOR'S NOTE

A FEW years ago I asked Daniel Mtusu, the subject of this book, to write for me an account of his life. He had completed it to a period a little beyond the time of his baptism, and was contemplating a further instalment when he died. His friend, the Rev. Andrew Mkochi, completed the story for me. I have rewritten in English what they have told me in their own language, and have added a certain amount of background to their pictures, so as to make them more intelligible to readers at home. I have followed throughout their account of events, and especially Daniel's own story of his youth and mental awakening.

My thanks are due to Rev. Charles Stuart, Miss Genner and to my wife for revising what I have written, and for many valuable suggestions. Rev. Alex. A. Russell has most kindly seen the book through the press, a work which I could not do personally, as I am in Nyasaland and my publisher in London.

My thanks are due also to Mr. Pierson of *The Missionary Review of the World* for permission to use the illustration of Daniel.

D. F.

PUBLISHERS' NOTE

THE life of Daniel Mtusu was originally intended to appear as an autobiography, but as this appeared unsuitable for the general reader the Author has rewritten it as a biography, but has retained all the spirit and essentials of the original.

CONTENTS

Contents

LIST OF ILLUSTRATIONS

Autobiography of an African

Chapter I

THE RED LAND & THE RED CHIEF

ARE DESCRIBED WITH SOME ACCOUNT
OF THE CHIEF'S STORMY END

THE Red Land, so called from the colour of its soil, is an undulating plateau more than four thousand feet above sea-level, lying to the west of Lake Nyasa. In the first half of last century it was a desirable country, covered with trees, well watered with numerous perennial streams and encircled by one goodly river, the Rukuru. Into this river all the water of the land flows, until it swells into a great flood. Two hundred miles from its source it plunges through a gorge in the mountains down to the mighty Lake in whose ample basin it is lost. To the east of the Red Land there rises a range of grass-covered hills, which separate the plateau from the hot shore-level of the Lake. From their cool heights south-east winds blow most of the year, lowering the temperature of the Red Land by several degrees.

A hundred years ago the wooded plateau was

B   17

studded here and there by patches of cultivation, where the natives had cut the trees and hoed their little millet fields. Close by these clearings stood rude villages, built of poles and mud and surrounded by a stockade of trees to defend them from sudden attacks of man and beast. The people who owned the villages and gardens were the Batumbuka, a backward, divided race, without a paramount chief and in constant feud with one another. They possessed fair herds of cattle and goats, and, living in a land with plentiful iron ore, many were black-smiths of some repute, who manufactured hoes, axes and arrow heads and sold them to surrounding tribes.

The Batumbuka were a dark-skinned, hairy race, of poor physique. Constant quarrels, with resulting scattering of the villages, bestial social practices, and the absence of any leader, and of any contact with higher races had allowed them to slide down the scale of civilisation until all pride of race and ambition were lost, and even their simple art of smelting iron was being forgotten through lack of power for social co-operation.

About eighty years ago a horde of wild savages suddenly burst upon this primitive and scattered people. Out from the long woods that stretched for hundreds of miles to the south they came like panthers, silently, suddenly. A little old man called Zungwendaba Jere led them, riding on an ox, for he was now lame through some disease in his knees. They were not a numerous people when they first appeared in the Red Land, but they were terrible in their cohesion and in the fashion of their weapons. A stern discipline knit them under one chief, though they had come out of many tribes, and, as their hand was against every man's, danger from the people whom they had harried cemented their unity. The men were all fighters, and were organised in regiments after the Zulu fashion. Their weapons were a short stabbing spear, a knobkerrie and a great ox-hide shield. Against these how feeble were the arrows that the Central African fired, even though they were tipped with poison! And who could stand against the devils when they charged in fearsome cock-feather head-dresses, yelling and brandishing their long-bladed assegais?

Plunder was their trade. From south of the Zambezi their track was marked by burned villages and emptied cattle-kraals. They hoed not, neither did they spin. The fields and barns of helpless villagers provided them with grain. The skins of antelope and goats were their garments, though some few were more softly clothed with a small strip of calico taken from native weavers or bought from Arab traders for stolen ivory. A huge mob of cattle, lifted from the tribes they raided, accompanied them, giving a supply of curdled milk and abundance of beef.

After two or three years of restless life in the Red Land, harrying the Batumbuka whom the new peril had gathered again into larger villages, they passed north and disappeared into the unknown, leaving behind them black, starving ruin. Tanganyika saw them. Their vanguard looked on the waters of Victoria Nyanza. Then they returned south.

One day they again poured down from the hills in the north into the Red Land. The old chief was dead, and a new one, called Mombera,* reigned in his stead, but he was followed by scarcely half the horde. Others had not acknowledged his succession, and were

* Really Umberwa.

now scattering over Central Africa by various routes, led by other claimants to power.

The Red Land, with its soil suitable for maize, its cool climate, its pasture land for cattle, and its blacksmiths who could make spears for the warriors, attracted the restless nomads. Along the banks of the Kasitu River they eventually settled and built their ramshackle villages, each with the circular cattle-kraal as the heart of all. North, south, east and west lay feeble tribes, possessing cattle and grain, an alluring and easy prey for the savages. Year by year, when the gardens were reaped, bands of warriors swooped down on these surrounding people and returned with strings of captives, a mob of cattle and loads of grain.

So the Abangoni (" the foreigners "), as this tribe was called, became the terror and the curse of Nyasaland. Readers of Livingstone's travels will meet them under various names, such as the Mazitu, the Baviti, the Batuta. Everywhere they stood for ruin and desolation.

Nor were they more friendly to the land of their settlement. Without forethought they hacked down the trees, and spread the branches over their gardens. These they burned when they were dry and so enriched the soil. Two years, or at the most three, finished the fertility of the ground, and another huge area of trees fell before the axes of their serfs. So the tree-covered land became rapidly deforested. The heavy tropical rains carried the loosened soil down the slopes and filled the river-beds, until the once loamy ground became hard, sun-baked and sterile, and the clear streams disappeared, leaving only waterless, sandy channels.

Unaccustomed to agriculture or to permanent

settlement, these nomads cursed the fair earth they had chosen as their habitation. Many a time the maize in their meagre, badly tilled gardens failed. There is no occupation so impoverishing as war, and every year saw semi-famine stalking through the land. Then hunger drove out the raiding bands again to seize the food of more careful cultivators.

Robbers, too, soon quarrel among themselves. Ambitious leaders with growing power would fain carve out kingship for themselves. Fifty years ago there lived such a captain among the Abangoni. His name was Chipatula Nhlane, and Hoho was his headquarters. He belonged to the Amaswazi nation in South Africa, and his father and he had followed the fortunes of the raiders through all their long wanderings. His company of robbers kept as their special hunting-ground the fisherfolk who live on the borders of Lake Nyasa and are known as the Atonga. Gradually, through continuously successful raids among their hamlets, he gathered together a great number of these folk as his serfs, and they formed the population of his rapidly growing villages.

He was a little, red-skinned man of boundless courage and energy, and his ambition grew with his possessions. By and by he added to his harem, as chief wife, a young sister of the reigning chief Mombera, and thereby increased his prestige and standing in the tribe. But, though children were born to his royal wife, all save one daughter died early, and the other head-men denied him the honour which they gave to the royal blood alone. His multitude of undisciplined serfs were among the most troublesome elements of the population. Over them the great chief Mombera had little control, and his scurrilous tongue invented many an ugly name for

them, the most polite being "The Rats of Hoho."
They quarrelled and fought with the villagers of other
head-men. They raided districts that were tributary
to other Abangoni. And there were no more cruel
fighters than the very serfs who themselves had been
carried captive and gradually incorporated into the
fighting ranks of the tribe.

Meanwhile the little red warrior grew in power
and became a chief to his own people. Brothers,
cousins, uncles were made village head-men and
guardians of his cattle and serfs. Their impudent
assertiveness knew no bounds, and by subtle impo-
sitions they gained wealth and position to which they
had no hereditary right.

So the Hoho people were feared and hated more
than any other section of the tribe, and much strength
and blood were spent in fratricidal fights.

Among the Abangoni family morality was fairly
high, and fearful punishments were meted out to the
adulterer. But when the sin was against a member of
the chief's household death was the invariable penalty,
and sometimes death was preceded by terrible cruelty.
With such a course of justice no one found fault, for
all knew that wrong done to the chief would be
visited in some subtle way upon the people. Magic
is one of the guardian angels of kingship. It was in
their own interest that they held the royal family as
peculiarly sacred property. Loyalty to the blood
royal, too, is deeply ingrained in the African and will
call forth the most sacrificial service.

When it was rumoured that a man named Bongo
had been tampering with a sister of Mombera, the
anger and energy of Chipatula, as well as his pride
in his relationship through marriage, drove him to
assume the responsibility of tracking down the alleged

The Red Land & the Red Chief

criminal and of avenging the insult laid upon the family with which he was allied.

Summoning a party of fighters he started off with them for Ekwendeni, whither Bongo had fled for his life. There they slept in an old village, and Chipatula used a hut which was infected with the tampan bug. He was badly bitten and a few days after lay in high fever. His people carried him back to his own village to break the magical spell that was on him. Nothing, however, could save him, and there he died.

There was a prodigious funeral. Thousands of people came to mourn, so that the sound of the wailing filled the valley. A great pit was dug in the cattle-kraal of the chief's head village, and four tunnels were scooped out from the foot of the pit. Into these were put his personal possessions and everything he had handled, and then his body, tied up in the skin of an ox, was laid among his goods. The men stood up, their shields and spears held behind their heads, and they wept with a heart-rending wail for the dead chief. All over the village hundreds of women sitting on the ground sang in melancholy cadences their bitter sorrow. To this sad music the grave was filled up.

Meanwhile messengers had been despatched to Mombera to report the death of his brother-in-law. "He died following after Bongo, who wronged your sister," reported the messengers.

Then the wrath of the great chief burst forth, and he demanded the death of Bongo. No further proof was necessary, for had not the accused fled, and was not magic hounding his steps, for already a great man had fallen? So Bongo was seized, together with his wives and dependants, who were all clubbed to death. But the chief culprit must not die so easily. He was

The Red Land & the Red Chief

tied to a stake and the dry wood was heaped about him. The fire was lit, and the people sat down to watch him burn. In his agony he cried, "You burn me, but what about Sango Chipeta ? "

"Hear him ! " shouted the Atonga slaves. "He accuses Sango. Sango, too, must die."

Off started the hunt, and Sango was seized, together with his chief wife, and they were added to the tale of victims that must avenge Chipatula's death.

Thus he who had filled his villages with slaves to hoe his gardens and fight his battles passed to the under-world with a train of spirits to serve him there.

Now Chipatula had been working for his own ends, and his frustrated ambitions had made him bitter against the other head-men of the Abangoni. In his umbrage he had said once to some of his Atonga slaves, "When I die, return to your own land at the Lake. There will be no one to hold you back."

This word was remembered, and was repeated among the slaves. Some of the more daring began to plan a sudden flight to the lands from which they had been torn. But this uneasy secret leaked out and somehow came to the ears of the Abangoni masters. In dealing with insurrection there was no mercy in their method. When Baza rebelled along with his Batumbuka people, the Abangoni hunted them to the top of Hora Mountain, and sat about the only path that led to this precipitous rock till they starved them to death. The timid who crept down to surrender were slain without pity. Ruthlessness was the motto of these savage rulers.

An order went forth, " Kill all the cows and bulls, but spare the calves and heifers." The meaning was plain. The grown men and women were to be massacred before they could escape, but the young people were to be saved, for the children could not act alone, and they could be trained into good servants.

For the slaves this was no time for hesitation. Word was passed round, and suddenly in the night the Atonga rose in rebellion under the leadership of Chinyenta. They slew the head-men and their free wives who were in charge of the villages, and then raced for Lake Nyasa and for freedom. In the morning, when the villages awoke, behold! the Atonga centres were deserted and the head-men were lying dead in their huts. But already the fugitives were miles away, and next day were welcomed within the stockaded villages of their relatives and friends by the shore of the great Lake.

The Abangoni lost no time in calling out three regiments of fighting-men to follow after and bring back the rebels. By three various routes they started off over the hills. On the way the regiments which came from Mombera's villages, marching by a southerly route, passed near certain villages of the Abangoni with which they had a quarrel. The opportunity for private revenge could not be overlooked. A fierce fight took place which left the attacking regiments broken and beaten. In headlong flight they returned to their own place.

The other two bands marched directly east and arrived before the great stockaded town of Chintechi. Their approach was not observed, and they hid in the woods during the night. But the Atonga were well aware that avengers would soon follow after the escaped slaves, and they had hidden defences in the marshes and dug carefully concealed pits in the approaching paths.

The Red Land & the Red Chief

When the dawn began to break the two regiments stood to arms and at a word from the general charged with wild yells through the marsh and along the paths. The marsh opened and seized them. The paths yielded, and men went headlong into pits where sharpened stakes impaled them. Then the great gates of the stockade were flung wide, and out flowed the Atonga, who knew their own defences. Soon the regiments were decimated, and but few survivors escaped back to the hills.

That was the Flodden of the Abangoni army. Up on the plateau the wailing in all the villages for sons and husbands and fathers who would never return is remembered to this day. The flower of the tribe lay dead in the marshes about Chintechi and the record for resistless victory had gone. To one of the wives of chief Mtwaro a child was born at this time, and she was called Balekile (the *impi* has fled). For many a raid thereafter heavy prices in lives were paid, and oftener now parties of slaves slunk off secretly in the night and made for the homes of their ancestors.

Chapter II

THE CHILD

WHO IS TO GROW UP BEFORE US IS INTRODUCED, AND
THE WHITE STRANGERS WHO FRIGHTENED THE
WARRIOR

NOW though Chipatula's head wife had no living sons, his other wives were more fortunate, and a considerable number of sons and daughters were left behind to inherit the wealth and power their father had gained. Among these was a lively little boy named Mtusu, born perhaps about 1870. Unlike most Central Africans, his skin was copper-coloured after the type of his Amaswazi forebears. His regular features were lit up with mischievous dark eyes. His neat, well-formed body seemed to be set on springs and capable of endless energy. Boys of his own age were always in his company, and he was their fearless, merry leader in every sport and adventure from which neither dirt nor danger deterred them, but rather added zest to the fun.

From the days when he left the goat-skin in which he was tied to his mother's back and was able to run about he was a child of the village. Its open public life was his nursery and home, though in his mother's hut there was a mat on which he might sleep and at his mother's fire was cooked the porridge which fed him. His playmates were the boys of his own

The Child

age, some of them half-brothers, others the children of his father's serfs.

Now and then little taboos interfered with his conduct as a chief's son and preserved his position. In the evening when the mothers, or slave girls, had prepared the evening meal, Mtusu was not allowed to eat with the other village boys. He must eat only with chiefs' sons, or other members of his family. Dishes of dried fish were sometimes prepared by the Atonga serfs, who longed for the cherished food of the days long ago when they lived by the Lake shore. But Mtusu must not eat fish, for the Abangoni said they were like snakes. Delicious stewed fowls were added as relish for the porridge, but these, too, were forbidden to Mtusu, for the domestic hen was of the same breed as crows. Beef was the true relish for children of a pastoral people.

Once a day in normal times he got a full meal of maize porridge, which only finished when his little stomach was so distended that it could hold no more. Then movement became slow and careful. Throughout the day, however, there were titbits for the hungry boy. Sometimes thick milk which had lain for days in an unclean gourd was poured into a dish, and the boys ate with their fingers. Again, a handful of maize roasted over the fire in a fragment of a broken pot, or a thick chunk of ground-nut pudding, was given to the boys. In season stalks of sorghum were brought by the women from the garden, and the boys tore off the outer bark with their teeth, as they sat or played about, and munched the inner core into pulp, sucking the sugar from it and spitting out on the ground the rejected fibre. They littered the village and paths with the sheath and white

The Child

fibre, greatly adding to the general untidiness, till ants and other scavengers cleaned up the refuse in course of time.

These were good days when there was plenty to eat. But hungry times fell upon the village every year. While there was grain in their barns the improvident villagers ate and drank without thought of the morrow, though experience might have taught them that their gardens were too small to last out the year. Then when they waited the harvest time with empty barns they lay dozing to forget their hunger, or gathered wild fruits and roots in the woods.

As a little boy Mtusu slept in his mother's hut, curled up on a reed mat, with his feet towards the fire, and a blanket of bark-cloth or dressed cowskin thrown over him. From dark till dawn he lay in unbroken sleep, and when the cold, grey morning wakened him he tumbled out of the hut without any preliminaries. No time was spent in dressing, for his only clothes were a string about his waist. He washed only when it was convenient, and in the cold season it never was. His little red body became covered with the earth of the village, and when the wind blew on cloudy days he shivered under a cake of dirt that coloured him a mottled grey.

There was no school to claim his time, no Sunday to mark the weeks. The phases of the moon were his sole calendar, and the coming of the rains was his New Year.

Each day at sunrise the bigger boys lifted the bars at the gate of the cattle-kraal. They milked the cows into dirty wooden vessels, and went forth with the whole herd to the pasture-ground, leaving the smaller children to play within the village and live their own

29

The Child

life. There the little ones made mud pies, and shaped rude models of oxen with clay and dried them in the sun. Just outside the village they set up little huts made of branches, and played at being grown men and women. They made spinning-tops with a round shell of a broken calabash through the heart of which they fixed a stem of grass, and sent their tops whirling towards slender goals of reedy grass. They danced war dances like their elders, holding a stick in their hands in lieu of a spear, and leaped about defying the chorus circle with eyes that blazed with simulated rage.

The aimless day slipped quickly into the cool evening and meal time. Stories were told about the fire till the little ones yawned and crept through low doors into the huts to sleep till morning. But when the moon was full for a time they joined their elders, who practised the *ingoma* dance within the kraal, and then slept to the music of the thundering feet and defiant song of the dancing men.

Mtusu was about eight years old when his father Chipatula died. He then passed under the guardianship of an uncle. For a year his mother wore the widow's cap of woven grass and hung on her neck the widow's weeds of endless strings of twisted bark. Dirt and neglect were the signs of sorrow, so she did not wash or beautify her body, and the village, too, grew more filthy and unkempt.

At last the mourning ended with a great feast of beer and dancing. The villages were broken to pieces, and the people moved away to the Kasitu Valley, where they built for themselves new dwellings. The kraal beneath which the dead chief lay buried was left standing in the midst of a dreary ruin. Some of the poles with which it had been built, striking root,

The Child

grew into little trees that sent forth leaf-bearing branches. The old village site was soon a desolation of dismantled huts and broken pots. But when the rainy season came a dense growth sprang up on the soil, which had been enriched by a few years of insanitary residence. So the dead chief lay in the midst of a thicket of luxuriant life.

After this came the rebellion of the Atonga serfs and the terrible disaster that attended the effort to bring them back. Sad, helpless months ensued for the Hoho people. Few men were left in the villages to keep the place tidy. Desolation and dissolution grew apace in this land of rapid life and rapid decay. The huts, never very substantial at best, began to fall to pieces. Poles rotted, white ants devoured. The loose thatch was blown from the roof, the grass grew thick and high in the villages, giving safe cover for snakes. The gardens were untilled for lack of men, and weeds sprang up and choked the grain. Hunger began to stalk through the land, and the helpless people looked on the growing desolation without heart or power to save themselves.

The fruits of plunder, too, were lacking, for raiding had received a wholesome check. The little cloth that was in the villages had gone to pieces, so that the naked people had no clothing save the few goat or buck skins they hung about their loins. White maize porridge seldom appeared now in the evenings. Mtusu and the other children had to satisfy themselves with the husks of maize steeped in water, or with what wild fruits they could gather in the wood.

One day the head-man of Chipatula's villages called together all the remaining warriors and said to them, " See, the children are dying for lack of

The Child

food. But down at the great Lake the Atonga are fat and eat from full barns. Let us forage there and get food for our children."

Eagerly the villagers prepared for war and the regiment assembled, ready to go forth. The great witch-doctor was summoned and, after consulting his bones, prophesied that the expedition would be prosperous, but warned them not to pass Chipatula's grave, which lay on their route, without making sacrifice there, for his spirit must be propitiated so that he might bless his children in the fight.

They marched forth with loud boastings, came to the lonely grave in the midst of the deserted village site and there made sacrifice. In the evening they reached the edge of the woods and built their booths there, intending to cross next day the wide, open grass-lands, cold and wind-swept, that separate the Red Land from the valleys and plains of the Atonga.

Early next morning one of the warriors went forth to look for hemp in the old village sites. He had been wandering about for some time when suddenly he came to a full stop, for there, standing among the trees, was a cloth house, and beside it were seated two white men and a black man. A little way beyond a number of native carriers were gathered round their wood fires.

The Europeans were Dr. Laws and Mr. Stewart, c.e. William Koyi, a Kaffir teacher from Lovedale in South Africa, accompanied them. They had come up to see the chief of the Abangoni and make friends with him, with a view to future extensions of missionary work. To the startled warrior they were only an apparition.

He stood staring in helpless wonder. Then Koyi spoke in the tongue of their fathers, for he, too, had

The Child

come from the land which their fathers had left years ago in the great restless adventure.

" Come near," he said, " for we are friends." But the robber would not approach, however reassuringly Koyi spoke.

" Go back," then cried Koyi, " and tell your friends the Abangoni that we are coming to visit them."

Quickly the man ran through the wood until he plunged into the midst of the regiment. " Silence everyone ! " he stammered. The noise of endless talk ceased and a great quiet reigned. The warriors looked up at the speaker, but he stood there in a maze, unable to utter a word. They questioned him, but no answer came. He stood as one whose brain reeled under a terrible shock.

At last he spoke slowly, " I have seen spirits of the dead. One of them seems a little familiar, and there are living Atonga with them. I tried to look carefully, and think that perhaps one is Chipatula, and another his younger brother who is dead. But they have living Atonga with them."

" Come," cried the warriors, " let us draw near and see."

So they cautiously approached the tent, and were received with great friendliness. The white men showed them their treasures, a little looking-glass and other trifles. Mr. Stewart placed a paper on a tree and fired at it in quick succession with his revolver, piercing the paper again and again. The awe and dread of the warriors were only increased by this timely demonstration, and, after a few yards of calico and some beads had been distributed among them, they took their departure.

Back at their own bivouac they discussed the vision. Some cried, " Are they not living men ? "

The Child

But others said, " They feel like spirits. See, they have just come from the grave. We touched their bodies and they are soft."

Runners were sent back to prepare the village for the coming of the white men. They burst on the surprised people, crying :

" The *impi* (regiment) has seen a great vision. Tell the witch-doctor to make the village ready, for strangers are coming."

Then the specialist of the spirit world set to work with ardour. Roots were pounded, mixed and boiled. Every house was asperged with the magic medicine. A place was chosen where the tent should be pitched and the site was thoroughly sprinkled. The villagers were called together and everyone was washed with protective magic. The children, too, were hidden away lest evil should come to them from the spirits who were on their way.

" The strangers have shown themselves to us men," the warriors said, " but you will be terrified at the sight of them. Their bodies are like the bodies of little children and are the colour of white calico. They seem like fish risen from the Lake. They gave us cloth and beads. The famine is now at an end."

At length the white men arrived, and the carriers pitched their tent at the appointed place within the village. All day long men stood and sat at a distance looking on the wonder that had come to the village, but the children were hid away and sat cowering in dark huts. Little Mtusu, however, was more curious than the others. He feared the magic of the white men as much as any, but he must see for himself what they were like. Creeping out of his hut, he slid round to where the crowd stood, and, lying on

The Child

his face, he peered through between the legs of the men and there saw for the first time the white people whose message was to have great results in his life.

This visit of the Europeans was a very short one. Next day they returned to the Lake, pleased with their reception, and planning for an early occupation.

Chapter III

THE HERD-LAD

IS HERE SEEN TRAINING FOR WAR BY FEARLESS AND SAVAGE FIGHTS WHILE FOLLOWING THE CATTLE

THE pride and glory of the Abangoni are their cattle. There is little other wealth among them. Years after this story begins, when the country was settled, Europeans have wandered through the land wondering what promises were here for them. Prospectors for gold have come, one after another, each hoping for the success which others failed to find, and have left hating the uninviting plateau. Twenty years ago and more, dragging with him weighty iron implements, there appeared among us a little Cornish miner. Doggedly he climbed the rocky kopjes and washed the sandy rivers, until one day he came down from a hill a raving madman and was carefully escorted out of the colony. The story spread that his sanity toppled before the sight of untold wealth in the rocks of that hill, and the natives nursed the story. Yet none of the restless prospectors who braved insanity to find his fabulous ore have seen trace of fortunes here. I gravely fancy the golden sun had struck him, not the vision of sudden wealth.

Planters have trudged back and forward, and seen that labour is abundant and cheap, but the soil is poor and unpromising. No tobacco or cotton can

The Herd-lad

grow here that would make cheap labour remunerative. So they have left without plans for bungalows set in the midst of great estates.

But adventurous pioneers have come this way, and bought for a mere song scores and scores of cattle, till they drove south a mob of them which they sold and made money sufficient to set themselves up in a farm or mine in Southern Rhodesia, where they soon lost all they had gained. Then Government stepped in and said enough cattle had been bought ; permits, difficult to obtain, were necessary for those who would export. Afterwards came East Coast fever and closed the land yet more effectually.

In the bad old days, before rinderpest had thinned the herds, thousands of sleek beasts stood in the open cattle-kraals and were tended and prized almost more than human beings. They had been gathered from droves that browsed in lands from the Zambezi to Victoria Nyanza, and the mixture had produced a large and useful breed. The sight of the evening was the long string of cows which came lowing home, as the herd-lads drove them to the village with shout and song and with the music of reed pipes.

The men loved to sit on the ground in the cattle-kraal and look on the village treasure, discussing the merits of each beast. They knew them all, and their language is rich in names for every variety. The red cow has its own name, and the black cow, the white, and the brindled and the spotted one. Huge oxen towered above the other beasts, bred for the sacrifice or the feast. A mighty bull, with heavy shoulders, a swaying hump and hanging silky dewlap, stood on the top of the great ant-hill round which the kraal was built and from this vantage-ground lazily surveyed his numerous wives, while he swished aside

The Herd-lad

the flies with flicks of his tail. The little calves were housed in the huts of the people, while the bigger ones were crowded into an open pen built by the side of the kraal.

In the dry season the ground of the kraal was covered with a fine, dusty manure that gave the young men a most suitable dancing floor for their energetic *ingoma*, and provided a soft comfortable seat for the elders during their long conversations. Here, too, sat the village court and all the idlers and witnesses, whose constant pleasure was to be present through those long-drawn-out cases. Here, too, gathered the councillors and the warriors, who sent the dust flying in suffocating clouds when they dashed into their wild war-dances.

But when the rains came the kraal was trampled into a quagmire in which the cattle stood up to their bellies in manure and mud. Then the people gathered outside the kraal under some shelter where they had drier surroundings.

The older lads used to herd the cattle, for out in the pasture glades there was plenty of danger and excitement. Lions prowled in the thick bush seeking the succulent wild pig, but ready, too, for a more substantial meal of beef. Leopards sprang out on the bigger calves that strayed too far. Sometimes, too, herds of rival villages came into collision. Then beasts and men fought together and the stronger won.

Mtusu has now reached the age for herding. One day he will be master of all the cattle in this village, for he is his mother's eldest son. Tacitly the other lads acknowledge him as leader. They are not slow to follow when his fiery, restless spirit provokes adventures. Though he is smaller in stature than most of his equals in age, none will beat him in daring

The Herd-lad

and endurance. See him one fine morning standing by the kraal gate driving the cattle forth. His copper-coloured skin shines in the light of the golden-faced sun. Two monkey skins hanging at his loins are his sole clothing. He holds in his left hand a small ox-hide shield and one or two knobkerries and a light spear. In his right he flourishes another knobkerrie which he brings down on the back of a cow to hasten its exit through the narrow gate, and all the while, with tongue between his teeth, keeps up an exciting whistle. Now the cattle have all gone through and are slowly moving towards the river glade where they will browse. No artificial foods will supplement the grazing of the day, yet the grass is very dry and unattractive in the uplands, while down by the river it is very scanty, though green and fresh. Big reaches of reeds, however, give plenty of good feeding.

Seated on the top of a high ant-hill Mtusu and his companions indolently watch the herd wandering about the open spaces before them. Suddenly a startled quail breaks cover. Immediately the boys are after it. It soars with a cry of alarm, and a dozen clubs fly into the air in an effort to strike it. The cattle are forgotten, and the chase goes on until at last the bird is brought to earth. A fire is started by friction, and soon the plucked quail is roasted and divided among the herd-lads.

As the day wears on the cattle are driven farther to fresh pastures. They are slowly pushing their way among the reeds when other cows begin to stray among them, coming from another direction. The herd bull looks jealously on the strange bull, and soon the noise of a struggle is heard. The guardians of the separate droves run in to turn the contending

The Herd-lad

animals aside. But they no sooner look on one another than fire darts from their eyes. The strange lads do not belong to the Hoho group of villages. Mtusu does not wait to count his enemies, but with a war-cry leaps into the fray swinging his club with deadly intent. His comrades rally round him, and in a few minutes there is a battle royal. Clubs swing and strike, shields are played for protection and passions are blazing. Now one or two have fallen and are lying sorely hurt among the reeds. Their companions run and leave the cattle to take care of themselves, but Mtusu and the other lads are after them like dogs after a fleeing cat.

At last the chase is over, and Mtusu rounds up the deserted herd, mingles it with his own, and, as the sun sinks in the west, he conducts all together home to his own kraal.

As the increased drove reaches the village with noise of much lowing and the whistles and war songs of the triumphant lads, all the people turn out and catch the prevailing excitement. Mtusu gives his account of the wild battle and flight. He has no regrets, neither have the men whose village has been so enriched. But they know well that the incident has not ended there, and preparations begin against the revenge.

Next morning the sun has scarcely risen when an armed party is seen approaching. But they are not allowed to come nearer. Mtusu's uncle and seniors have recognised the avengers who have come to claim their raided herd. At once they issue forth with spears and clubs to defend themselves. Out there in the open space there is another fierce fight and the attacking party is driven back. There is only one redress now for the losers. They go to the great chief,

Mombera, and lay their complaint before him. He murmurs impatiently scurrilous words about the "Rats of Hoho" and appoints a day when the case will be tried.

When the day arrives the Hoho men are there from all their villages, armed to the teeth, and they sit in a cluster on one side of the great kraal of the royal village. The accusers are there, too, in full force, supplemented by many friends who are gathered together on the opposite side of the kraal. The great chief Mombera, seated with his councillors on the ground, faces the kraal gate. He is a little black-skinned man. A strip of blue calico lies loosely about his loins, or slips to the ground leaving him stark naked. A leopard skin forms his throne, and by his side stands a gourd filled with foaming beer.

The trial goes on with much calmness. Speaker after speaker rises to his feet and talks with dignity and fluency. The whole case seemed so plain and simple, but soon it is covered with a mass of complications. Old incidents of the past generation are brought forth and somehow related to this recent fight. As the discussion proceeds, sometimes breaking into fiery passion, the chief seems entirely uninterested. The gourd is raised constantly to his mouth, and his whole face is hidden behind its great bulk; but the watcher can see a supercilious eye looking round one side of the gourd and measuring the speaker who is on his feet. At length the chief gives judgment. In a few caustic words he declares the Hoho people guilty and orders them to restore the stolen cattle. The people shout "Bayete." They have accepted the decision, and for the present the matter is ended.

The Herd-lad

No words of reproof are given by the elders to Mtusu and his hot-heads. For this is the stuff that makes warriors who will enrich the tribe, and after all most of their possessions have been gained by might, and not by right. But it is a dangerous society that is being built on unbridled passions. Life has no sacred value, and robbery is not long scrupulous about the honour of an open fight against equal numbers. Killing was a brutal and sordid game for the Abangoni, and most of their boasted raids were cowardly butcheries of helpless people. So the idle herd-lads, thirsting for the exciting life of the full-blooded warrior, became the terrors of the path.

One day the herdsmen were sitting on the ant-hill while the cattle browsed near at hand. All about spread a thick tangle of bush land through which ran a winding track. In some thinning of the scrub the lads spied a solitary traveller. He was carrying a little load of no value. Behind him there seemed to be one or two companions straggling some distance off. The spirit of mischief was bubbling in the lads, and one of them was told to go down and speak to the stranger. Off ran one or two reckless fellows and waited by the side of the path. As the solitary wayfarer approached they saluted him courteously and asked for a snuff. He was suspicious, but could only respond quietly before superior numbers. So he laid his load on the ground to get his snuff-box from his waist-band. The herd-lads snatched at his bundle and tried to make off with it. He struggled to keep his property, but they knocked him on the head with a knobkerrie. At this moment his companions arrived, and rushed to the rescue of their friend.

From the ant-hill the waiting lads charged down,

The Herd-lad

and soon there was a wild scrimmage. One of the travellers recognised the party and shouted out that the assailants were Hoho villagers. On hearing this the cry was raised that it must be a fight to the death, for they had been recognised and would be accused. Blood flowed ; clubs and spears were used with murderous intent, and before long the wayfarers were all lying dead in the bush. The herd-lads then drew the bodies farther into the thick tangle of scrub and left them well hidden there. They knew now that their secret was safe and that no one was left to accuse them.

Considering the perils of herding, it was no wonder that only the bigger lads were sent out with the cattle.

In the evening when they returned with their charges the less said about the events of the day the better for everyone. But the elders knew well that all had not been quiet and decorous out in the river glades while they sat over the beer pot. What did it matter, provided only the cattle came back with numbers undiminished when the sun went down ? They, too, had the faculty of preserving a discreet silence.

When the moon was shining, the nights were full of healthy sport. Then the cattle stood silently in one crowded section of the great open pen, while men and women filled the rest with energetic dance. The men with dancing sticks in their hands and little bunches of feathers tied to their head stood in a large semicircle singing a manly, defiant song, and thumping with tremendous thrusts of their feet the loose, dry dung that made their dancing floor. The women minced in front of them carrying long wands in their hand and singing a shrill chorus that blended with

The Herd-lad

the men's song. All over the valley resounded the loud song of the various village dances which continued far into the night, till the performers turned into their huts to sleep, wet with perspiration which flowed over bodies covered with the dry dust of the kraal.

Chapter IV

THE HOUSE-BOY

FINDS THE RESTRAINT AND QUAINT MANNERS OF THE EUROPEAN VERY TRYING

THE first visit of the Europeans was duly reported to Mombera, and communications were established, further visits paid, and at last two Kaffir teachers were sent up to open work among the Abangoni. Shortly afterwards Dr. Elmslie arrived, and then his young wife. They built a station under Njuyu mountain neighbouring the Hoho group of villages. For years their presence was barely tolerated by the war leaders, though Mombera himself was friendly. School work was not permitted at first, for the head-men were quick to recognise that the teaching of the schools would be opposed to a life of marauding.

All the time, however, refining influences were working unobtrusively, for the doctor and his wife had set up a Christian home in this most savage and homeless land. A goodly-sized house was built with bricks and mud. The roof was thatched with grass, the floor was brick, the light and air of heaven streamed in through swinging doors and glazed windows, making the large whitewashed rooms bright and fresh. The smoke of the fires did not blacken the interior and make the eyes smart, for it found its way mysteriously through chimneys into the open

45

air. Reed mats served for carpets, chairs and tables were made from boxes and from planks sawn out of local timber. White and coloured cloths lying here and there on tables and chairs gave brightness and daintiness to the rooms.

What months of hard work were necessary before such a home was formed! Men and women who had never done other than their own simple village work had puddled ant-hill clay and moulded bricks. Trees had been drawn from the hill by gangs of warriors and adzed into rough planks. Doors and windows had been fashioned in the carpenter's shop at Bandawe and carried up to the hills. For there had been no lack of labour so long as the white men were willing to pay in cloth week by week. Even while they worked and returned home with scraps of grey calico there stole upon the villagers some sense that labour was more remunerative than war, and that though they might dispute the European's teaching, his presence at least enriched them.

Outside this home of Christian refinement drunken sensual paganism surged. The cattle, driven forth by their passionate herdsmen to browse on the scanty herbage, at times looked on with big solemn eyes at cruel robbery and fierce encounters. Now and again a raiding band in full war-paint could be seen passing out to do mischief, or returning with whitened bodies laden with the spoils they had seized. In the royal kraal beyond the river endless cases occupied the hours of most days of the week, or wild war-dances full of defiance and threatenings excited the people. The noise of great beer carousals could be heard at times, and the maudlin song of the drunkard returning home at night in vociferous company whose shouting chased away threatening spirits and lurking beasts of prey. The sounds of the great dance floated up from the valley every clear moonlight night.

In the little parlour of the mission house a lamp was burning, shining on the bookcase near which the doctor was reading and on the white garments the gentle wife was sewing. Their home seemed but a feeble light in the dark night that wrapped the land. The Christian worship that daily sanctified the house seemed to be limited to the range of the four white-washed walls; the testimony of their life and work but a whisper in the tumult of paganism. The peace and refinement and faith of the Gospel had to be sought for. In all this wide land it was nowhere to be found except within that little Christian mission house.

Within its shelter two or three young savages were acting as domestic servants, receiving unconsciously lessons of cleanliness and order and Christian courtesy, sharing day by day in the subtle atmosphere of family worship, and learning somewhat unwillingly the mysteries of the alphabet, the key to reading. Their lessons were not taught without sore strain on the lady of the house, nor without sulky rebellion against the new discipline and morality to which they were subjected. Lying, pilfering and dirt were innocent enough habits in the village, but were heart-breaking vices in the mission house, forbidden and punished. Care and tidiness, truth and diligence, were virtues to be learned by unwearied following.

It was a patient waiting ministry this. But it paid a thousandfold. To-day many of the native ministers and senior evangelists will tell you that it was in similar Christian homes that the message of the Gospel first touched them, threw its arms about them and enfolded them.

The House-boy

Bright, active Mtusu was one of these fortunate house-boys. His uncle was ambitious for him, and was wise enough to recognise that the white man had riches to give worth having. Anyone could see the attraction of this quick lad, and the missionaries added him to their staff. He washed the dishes, and broke them, too. He made the bed in the morning and swept the room, puzzled with the Europeans' horror of dirt and zeal for clean tidiness. He stood by at table when they ate, heard the doctor acknowledge God at each meal, and watched his courtesy to his wife, especially wondering that a man should eat along with a woman and give her the honour in all things.

Everything was strange to him ; the house and all its furniture were marvels of ingenuity and boundless wealth. The habits of the white people, so elaborate and particular, confused him, and made them seem a race so different from his. Why did they require so many dishes and other implements for eating? Why did they nibble food so, instead of taking full satisfying meals? Why should they hate dust that was almost invisible and wash their hands when they seemed so clean ? How delicate and fragile they were, and what great precautions must be taken for their comfort ! Sickness never seemed far from them. How constantly they lay sweating out their fevers !

When Mtusu went home to his village the people questioned him closely about all he saw, surprised that he should dare to live with the strangers. "They are not men and women like us," they said. "They are fish out of the Lake. You are silly to live with them."

But when he professed no fear, in their curiosity they asked him all about their ways of life. "Do

A CHIEF'S GRAIN STORE

they sleep as we do?" they asked. "What do they eat? Why do they not touch their food with their fingers? How can they live on such little morsels of food? Have they toes on their feet? We only see their boots." And so on the questions flowed. The answers were not always accurate and truthful, for the temptation to romance was over-strong. Queer and marvellous tales floated through the land which had originated in the brain of Mtusu, for the more wonderful the master was the greater was the reflex glory of the servant.

But Mtusu was not at ease, though he talked boastfully to his friends. Family prayers disturbed him badly. Every day the house-boys were called in to join the family circle, and, after the doctor had read a passage from Scripture, he and his wife knelt in prayer. He spoke to Some One Who was not visible, and he went on and on speaking. Mtusu could not understand much of what he said. This was the habit of madmen, to talk to themselves. If a villager acted so he would be set aside as insane, or as possessed by a spirit, and hounded from the village. Then the fear came upon Mtusu that he might learn the habit, and he, too, would become an outcast. At last, in spite of all his boldness, he could stand it no longer. The prayers were a terror to him. So he went to Dr. Elmslie and asked that he might be allowed to return home again.

The doctor would not hear of it, and his wife was greatly distressed. "We love to have you here," she said. "We do not wish you to go away."

But he urged more strongly that he must go, for the lady's eagerness to have him in the house only increased his fear.

"Wait," she said, "that I may teach you to read,

and some day you will be able to read as well as I can."

But he had no desire to read. Indeed, the written word was more terrible then than any sorcery. It was all a wonder, and those who found the magic which made a book speak must be the most dangerous of wizards. He determined that, no matter how they urged, he would escape before it was too late. Deception was evidently an easier path than open avowal, so he professed to be content and willing to stay.

Day by day he brooded over his danger. When the doctor asked him to join with them in prayer he closed his lips, shut his eyes and refused to utter a word. One day he asked to be allowed to pay a visit to his village, promising to return quickly. Permission was given, and his mistress added, "Come back in the evening."

Mtusu, however, had no intention of putting his foot within such a madhouse again. The free life of the herd-lad was more to his liking. Next morning the little bit of calico which made him a decent house servant was discarded, the skins hung again at his loins and, with knobkerrie and spear, he followed the cattle.

Two or three days went by, and when Mtusu did not return Dr. Elmslie sought him at the village and asked his uncle why his ward had left him. He urged that he should be sent back, knowing well how to appeal to the uncle's self-interest, and convincing him that Mtusu was on a surer road to greatness and wealth by learning to work than ever he would be in the company of the herd-lads.

To all this the sly old man readily assented, for he was well aware that what Mtusu received as wages would be properly divided among his relatives and

the uncle would have the lion's share. When Mtusu
returned with the cattle in the evening he was talked
to very seriously and ordered to go back to his house-
work.

Perhaps the few days' freedom had been good for
him and had let him see that already he was a lad
apart from his fellows. At any rate, he was soon
reconciled to life and work in the European house,
and began to learn more willingly the lessons that
were taught.

About this time the missionaries ventured to teach
more openly, and a little school was held on the
verandah of the dwelling-house. Only six lads
attended, but they were the brightest in the Hoho
group, and they dared the scorn of others that they
might learn the white man's knowledge. But the
hard work of steady application was most distasteful
to them. They demanded payment for the prolonged
exertion ; they absented themselves when they
wearied of the lessons or when any attractive dance
or expedition was organised at the village ; and too
often they irritated their patient teacher beyond
endurance by their impertinence.

Among the six Mtusu was now sitting, a restless
pupil. Mr. McIntyre was the European who initiated
them into the mysteries of letters. His hand had a
deformed finger, and one day he asked Mtusu, " What
is this ? " pointing to a letter of the alphabet. Mtusu
did not see the letter, but he did see the finger, and
he burst out laughing at the deformity. The teacher
rose angrily to punish him for his impudence, but he
darted aside and fled along the verandah into the house,
and, shutting the door, turned the key. Already his
house training had made him wiser than his fellows.

Dr. Elmslie was then called, and he sternly rebuked

The House-boy

the youth, telling him he must never again repeat his impertinence.

"Stick to your lessons," he said, "and learn everything your teacher tells you. Then you will find that you will eat good things, and you will be glad you listened."

Now a simple word in this sentence stuck to Mtusu. He pondered over it as he went back to the class. What did the doctor mean by the "good things" he should eat? Was it sugar, the sweetest of all things?

He talked it over with the other lads when he told them of the doctor's conversation.

"The Muzungu (white man) has told me not to laugh when I am being taught, for when I have learned he will give me good things. I think he means sugar, the white man's beer. I know what it is like, for when I washed the dishes I sometimes tasted it, and it is sweeter than honey."

Not yet had the young savage come to know that there is a knowledge "sweeter than honey," but in anticipation of a coming reward he and his fellows worked a little harder than before, and made some progress with their learning.

Chapter V

THE CONTEST

SCHOOL, however, was only an experiment. The great chief Mombera had been friendly to Dr. Laws and was a frequent visitor to Dr. Elmslie's house, where the Europeans' possessions, and especially Mrs. Elmslie's sewing machine, fascinated him. But he was not master of his own people —there were restless youths who longed for war, and councillors who saw no glory but in victorious raids. Again and again the chief was defied and mocked in the kraal because he allowed the missionaries to undermine the spirit of the people.

At length the hot-heads prevailed, and the council sent out word that the little verandah school must cease. They would not have the children wiser than the elders, or where would parental discipline be? And was not the school teaching peace instead of war, and turning the lads into cowards who could not fight?

Public preaching, however, was still continued in the village kraals. Before the Europeans had arrived or had acquired the language of the people, Koyi (whom the people called Mtusane) was able to speak in a tongue they understood, and his face was black like their own, though his dress was the dress of the

53

The Contest

European and his family was unknown. One Sunday he was preaching in the open kraal before a goodly concourse of men.

"Men, listen to my words," he cried. "Give over war, and what you seek we shall help you to find. Live in peace, and God will be with you, and you will be His people. Once I was such as you, but now I belong to God."

Such words were not acceptable. Murmurs of disapproval ran through the crowd, and some spoke out, "If a man calls the people together, is he to talk to them and receive no answer? Let us talk also."

Then up rose the orator Nkwelula and said, "Yes, we have heard. Some of the words are good, but you teach that God forbids us to war. There you lie. Whom are the people to fear? When were the Abangoni ever defeated? You say we shall receive the things we desire. Where are they to come from? How shall we get them if we do not take them? Listen, men, Mtusane lies when he says that God does not approve of war. In our wars we worship God. If He allows us, we destroy a stockade and take cattle and goats ; if He forbids, we are unable to enter the stockade. When He approves great is our fame among the people. So when Mtusane speaks of war he lies. But all he has taught about adultery and lying and theft is true. For we know that if a man is a thief or adulterer he will be killed when he goes to fight. There he speaks the truth ; but as for war, he lies."

That was sound theology and sound ethics to the Abangoni, and loud murmurs of approval ran round the kraal. It was well that someone should voice the national sentiment, for discussion is a much healthier

54

The Contest

thing than silent apathy. The difference between the Abangoni and the Christian missionaries was not one of faith, but of ethics. All the news the white men brought of God and immortality was good and welcomed. For Africa never doubted God. They knew Him as the author of life and of death, and that in some dim way He was mixed up with their doings. They never doubted that the spirit of man only inhabits his body, and when death comes to the body the spirit still lives and goes to the world of spirits. But all that was now being told them of the character of God and what conduct God demanded from those who worship Him was new, and much of it unacceptable.

To some of the commands they gave unqualified assent. The old men loved to hear the missionary press the fifth commandment, for strict obedience and reverence of the children for their elders were the foundation of their village life. Mtusu well knew that his guardians had power over him, even to scourgings were he disobedient. Love and reverence for mothers were among the most admirable of their virtues. Breaches of the seventh commandment were followed by fearful punishments, and the old men gave loud and violent assent to this command when it was read. But not to steal and kill were scarcely straightforward prohibitions. They must not steal from their fellow-villagers—that would be crime against their own society. To take the property of another tribe or village which was not of their own community was no offence at all. Mtusu could help himself to the white man's sugar, for the white man was a stranger to his society. But if he entered the hut of a villager, though there was no lock upon the door, and took from it a few ground nuts, that would be a fearful crime. The village needed no policeman to protect its property, for magic was a most effective guardian. Though no eye saw, magic had seen and was sure to follow with dire punishment. So, too, killing was no murder when you killed an enemy. In war killing was a necessary act, or you never could conquer and get your own way. When wrong was done, and men sinned against their own community, everybody knew that evil followed. Their feet began to swell from mysterious causes, the women had hard labour, disease visited the village, and defeat would be the lot of the " impi." But these penalties never followed violence which was done to enemies, or to people who were not bound up in their common village life.

The uncompromising teaching of the missionaries thus roused violent opposition, especially when it ran against the age-long practices of the people. Angry murmurs were uttered against those who were disturbing their tribal customs, and especially against the Hoho people, who had harboured the strangers and were profiting by their presence.

In the kraals men spoke to one another of their dark forebodings. " The Hoho people invited the white men in," they said, " now they are demanding their children. Wait a little. When the Europeans return to their own country they will carry away these Hoho children. Then the fathers will come to us and say, ' See, they have carried away our children.' But we will answer, ' Whose blame is it ? You invited them into the country.' "

Thus the cleavage between Hoho and the rest of the tribe became wider than before. Some lads continued to frequent the mission station, and, as the Europeans were making bricks and erecting

The Contest

houses, the villagers round about worked and received wages. Calico was more commonly seen in Hoho than in other villages, and everyone knew that Hoho was enriched by the presence of the white people. Mtusu and the other more prominent lads who were being initiated into better skilled labour were derisively nicknamed "The Bricks." When they would join in sport common to all the people they were hounded away with angry cries. "Clear off! We don't want to see the white man's folk. If we allow them, they will draw us also to be with them."

One of the mission followers was bold enough to join in a village dance. Shortly afterwards he was murdered on the path. Mtusu, along with others, tried to find out who had murdered their friend, but the people only jeered at them, saying, "Consult your books, and your white men. Their magic should be able to tell you who killed your friend. We won't."

Such evidences of hate and evil intention kept the little mission station in a condition of unpleasant tension, so that evil was suspected when none was intended.

One day, when Mtusu was setting out the table for a meal and the doctor was lying in bed very ill with fever, a mob of people went rushing past the house. Women and children ran for safety to Njuyu mountain, crying out that a war-party was on its way to kill the Europeans and the Hoho people who had befriended them.

Mtusu roused Dr. Elmslie, and, though he was very ill, he went out and, climbing an ant-hill, looked through his glasses. In the distance he saw a regiment on the march. It was not making for the mission house, however, but for another village of Hoho,

57

where it seized the cattle and goats and then returned to Ekwendeni, whence it had come.

The presence of the mission station was becoming an intolerable nuisance to the more restless spirits in the tribe. Peace was persistently taught while the position and wealth of the nation depended on continuous war. Again and again angry discussions broke out at the royal kraal, and violent head-men leapt into threatening war-dances defying the paramount chief. At length the enemies of the mission got the upper hand, and it seemed as if the Europeans would be forcibly driven out of the land. An army began to gather in the valley beneath the mission station, and Dr. Elmslie and his wife prepared for sudden flight.

The one treasure that the doctor could not afford to lose was his medicines. Secretly in the dead of night he dug a hole in the floor of one of the rooms, carrying the earth out in baskets, and after carefully pounding it he scattered it in the wind that no one might have a suspicion of the preparations he was making. On the bottles and tins he scratched the names of the medicines, so that when he hid them the white ants might not devour their identities. For all the time he knew that, when the rage had passed, he would return again, for God had not led him to claim the Abangoni in vain. So secretly were his arrangements made that even Mtusu and the other house-boys had no suspicion of what was being done in the darkness of night.

The gathering army dispersed, however, without taking any action, for counsels were still divided, and among the mission's most powerful friends were the great chief himself, and the eminent witch doctor whose sons were the first secret disciples.

The Contest

While the tribe was only being restrained from war by the blocking opposition of these friends, Dr. Laws arrived on a visit to Mombera. In the long discussion which followed in the kraal the wilder spirits demanded that the mission should leave Bandawe so as to give the Abangoni free opportunity to attack the Atonga, and that the missionaries should come to live on the hills so that the Abangoni might have a larger share in the wealth that came from their presence. A compromise was effected when an offer was made to open a new station in another section of the warrior tribe, and, after some talk when plain facts were put before the council, a peace was arranged and permission was given to open schools.

Chapter VI

WAR

THE Abangoni were well aware that with the sanctioning of schools they were allowing the entrance of a new force which would change the life of the people. Many of the old headmen who were wedded to war did not withdraw their opposition for many years. They consistently refused to allow schools within their sphere of influence, and looked with suspicion on the work of the teachers among their fellow-tribesmen. But a patch of land had now been granted on which the missionary might sow his seed and cultivate some tender plants. When these grew and germinated the winds of heaven would carry the seed over the whole land until the foreign plant of Christ's gospel of peace began to spring up in the most guarded and forbidden places.

But you do not suddenly alter the temper of a people and turn them from war to peace. You may restrain them from outbreaks by force of arms and the prohibitions of a strong Government. No European power had yet claimed these lands and overawed the raiding propensities of the people. The only protector was the " still, small voice " which now began to speak with mild suggestions and a constant reiteration, but there were few, if any, who heard it. Even the

War

few pupils who ventured to come to school were there, not to seek eagerly the new doctrine, but to learn to read, and acquire power for themselves.

Among the scholars who heard indifferently the daily Bible lesson, and a little more willingly trod the rough path that leads to knowledge of reading and writing, was the lad Mtusu. He had at length passed the initial difficulties and was able to read the gospels in his own tongue. But his mind was saturated with the wild stories of the fighting days, and he was still a lad of the people, following their customs and fired with their fierce ambitions. In the house he was a quick and intelligent servant and had gained some superficial knowledge of the white man and his ways. But this veneer of civilisation did not affect his attitude to tribal customs, and the lust of war was as deep in him as in any other normal lad.

So it came to pass that when he received a summons from the village head-men to join in a foray to the north his heart leaped with joy, and, forgetting the lessons of the household and of the school, he returned to his village.

The opportunity of this projected raid had been given by a native from the north end of Lake Nyasa who had escaped from justice and fled to the Abangoni. Moved by a desire for revenge, he offered his services as guide to the army if they would go and burn the villages from which he had fled.

The suggestion was too welcome to be ignored, and the war-heralds called from the ant-hills that food should be prepared for the expedition. Mtusu and the other young men now sharpened their spears, arranged their great head-dresses of cock feathers and danced impatiently in the kraals. At last the heralds announced the day of starting, and then Mtusu joined his regiment, fully arrayed. His bright eyes glowed fiercely beneath the huge bunch of feathers which adorned the head of an unmarried warrior. An assegai and club were his weapons of offence, and he carried a war-shield of ox-hide, big enough to cover his whole body.

When the regiments went forth they made a long detour, instead of heading straight for the north end of Lake Nyasa, lest reports of their objective should precede them.

One evening when they were building their sleeping-sheds a cobra was found in them. Here was an omen which must be interpreted, and that was done by the witch doctor who accompanied the army. After he had consulted his bones, he explained, " This is good luck. You will also find an elephant in a game-pit on the path that leads to the Lake. These are the spirits of Chipatula and his son, who go along with you."

In great hopes the regiment went on, glad that their father was with them ; and indeed next day they did find an elephant in a pit, whose tusks they cut off and carried with them.

As they drew near Karonga's village at the north end of the Lake, they travelled only by night so as to make a surprise attack, and at last arrived in position, in the faith that no one suspected their approach.

They lay hid in the thick bush just a few yards from the stockade and waited for the dawn. By and by the first grey light began to break, and with it they saw the old chief open the gate of the village and go forth to lift the stakes that had been laid on the path to make approach dangerous for a night attack. Gathering them all so as to leave a safe way

War

for his own people to go and come, he returned to the village, and soon appeared again with a pot of beer which he laid outside the gate where he and his friends were wont to drink and talk together.

Suddenly from the bush around there burst a fearful yell. Hundreds of wild savages in fearsome garb rushed out of the thick growth yelling and whistling, and in a moment were through the gate and tearing round the village. They stood by the doors of the huts waiting for the terrified people, so rudely awakened from sleep, to creep out from the low doors. There were girls, boys and men among the slain, but some were saved alive to be slaves to the Abangoni. Karonga, the chief, escaped to the hills. His village was fired and the cattle and goats were driven off to the booths where the robbers had spent the night. There the booty was divided, and the slaves were apportioned out among the captors.

Some of the poor people escaped along the Lake shore and took refuge in villages there, only to be attacked after two days' peace by the Ekwendeni regiments who burst on this district one fine morning and left other burning ruins behind them.

The journey home was made by a more direct route, and while the army was still on the road messengers were sent ahead to announce the victory. They arrived in the night and told the great chief and his head wife that the *impi* was approaching. Two or three days afterwards the formal entry was made. Every man who had slain a victim had plastered his face and body with white clay, and those who had only wounded plastered the right arm and one side of the face.

When the excitement of this expedition was over, Mtusu returned to school along with the other young

63

warriors whose education had been thus interrupted, but his household service had ceased.

The nation, which had again tasted blood, could not settle down. Within a few weeks the villagers were once more awakened from sleep by the shout of the war-herald. Standing on the top of the ant-hill in the cattle-kraal, his figure silhouetted against the grey dawn in the east, wearing the head-ring of the married warrior, with his left hand he raised aloft a great knobkerrie, and shouted in long-drawn syllables, " *Muyezwa-na ?* " *

A great hush fell on the awakening people, and they heard the call to the women to prepare meal for the army which was soon to go forth.

That day no pupils came to school. All was bustle and excitement in the villages. Women pounded maize, men sharpened their spears and renewed their head-dresses and other furnishings of war.

Sorora hill was the rendezvous where the regiments from all the tribe collected. After all had arrived Msukuma Ndhlovu, the great *induna* of the army, sent out his heralds to proclaim, " Muyezwa-na ? To-morrow we go forth."

Next morning the regiments defiled into the Berere marsh in two great strings. Between the files freeborn girls marched, laden with large calabashes of beer, and young lads with goat-skins filled with maize meal and prepared food. They had not gone far when a violent dispute arose, through the demand of the Hoho people that they should have precedence of the Embangweni group. But the *induna* decided the quarrel by sending the regiment of the royal village to the front and then alloting places to the others.

* " Do you hear ? "

YOUNG ABANGONI IN WAR DRESS

War

The Lundazi River was crossed near the place where the Government station now stands, and then they descended over waterless, stony hills to the great hot Loangwa Valley. Quietly they passed Kazembe's villages, doing no damage, for this chief paid tribute to the Abangoni. When a great herd of elephants met them, the witch-doctors who accompanied the army were called to interpret this omen.

"As great as has been the number of elephants which passed through the army," they said, "so great will be the band of captives that you will take. But let us sacrifice first to the spirit of our father, Zungwendaba, that he may lead to victory the army of his child."

That evening all the men gathered to worship. As they were now near the villages which they proposed to raid, the heralds proclaimed in the morning following, "Muyezwa-na? Cook now, for to-morrow the army will attack the stockade of Chipembere" ("the rhinoceros").

Then the air was filled with smoke from the fires of the army, for the booths in which they had slept stretched out in a straggling line for many miles. After they had eaten, they moved on and slept near the River Mongalozi, and when the cocks began to crow they flowed round the first outlying village like water.

Two men came through the gate at dawn going forth to hunt game. Right through the army which was hidden in the dense undergrowth they passed, suspecting nothing, for all waited silently the command to advance and had not yet begun to beat their shields. By and by the hunters caught sight of the dark shields of one of the crouching regiments, and, thinking they had spied a herd of buffalo, they began to creep

War

towards them to get a close shot with their guns. Suddenly they saw the general walking about among his companies, giving them their orders, and when it dawned on the hunters that the Abangoni were there they cried out. Then the general shouted, "Catch them!"

The army heard their leader's voice, and thought he had ordered them to assault. With one united yell and blowing on their pipes they rushed to the attack. The village was entirely unprepared, and made no defence. It was taken without much loss, only about ten of the Abangoni being killed. Mtusu had a narrow escape from an arrow, but successfully caught it on his shield.

Msukuma now ordered the army to withdraw, for there were still four stockades that they must assault and the river before them was full of crocodiles. Besides, they could now hear the beating of drums in Chipembere's town and the alarm cries of the women. So all the regiments were told to approach the chief's town.

By and by they sat down surrounding this stockade, on whose poles they could see human heads transfixed. These were the heads of Abangoni who had followed Mpezeni, an elder brother of Mombera, and chief of one of the sections of the tribe which had not acknowledged Mombera's succession. They, too, had attacked this town and had been completely defeated. Mtusu counted thirty heads from his position as he sat with his regiment.

When the general saw this ghastly sight he commanded the army to retire, lest their courage should ooze away as they sat and waited beneath these trophies.

Till about ten o'clock the warriors remained im-

66

patiently waiting the command to attack. Loud murmurs broke out among them, " Why have you left us sitting before those slaves? What are we waiting for? Why do we sit staring at one another? Let us fight at once."

An hour after the general ordered the army to stand up with their shields in their hands. Then he passed through the regiments, giving them their places, while they beat their shields and shouted their defiant war-cries, " Mosi Mo ! " " Mwana mwana Kwichi ! " " Nkabi ! Nkabi ! Nkabi ! "

At length he gave the order : " Charge as one man ! " With a terrific yell the regiments rushed forward. But out from the stockade burst a volley of gunfire. The bullets pierced the shields and bodies of the Abangoni. Men fell in all directions, and the assault was stopped before a single man had touched the stockade of Chipembere with his hands.

The general now ordered them to retire, and while they rested a little he worshipped again the great tribal spirit.

Another assault was ordered with a like deadly result. Three times they charged, only to retire broken and leaving their dead strewn about the stockade.

Again the general prayed to the tribal spirit, and then cried to the regiments, " Are you afraid? "

They shouted, " We fear nothing. We don't wish to see the heads of our men transfixed on the poles. Let us charge again, and if anyone wishes to run away he is no man of Mombera."

So they rushed with one mind up to the stockade. Some tore at the poles trying to open an entrance. Others scrambled up and over the high palisade, and in a few moments the Abangoni were within the village.

War

Now the fight was intense, and at close quarters, for the keen game-hunters of this town determined to sell their lives dearly.

Mtusu was in greater danger of death than ever he had been before. A bullet from a gun smashed his spear and passed through his left arm, but it had already spent its force and did not enter his body.

A vast number of men and women were slain in Chipembere's town, for the army had completely surrounded the place so that none escaped. The captives raised a great cry for the dead, and the victors remembered the cadences of that wail, and sang them as their song of victory when they returned to their own land.

The arrival of the army was a great event. When Mombera heard the report of the first messengers he smeared his body with black and white magical medicines and came forth to greet his victorious warriors. In the great kraal the general told again the story of the fight, and then named the heroes who had distinguished themselves. The first who entered the stockade was the hero of all. To him was given a great ox. The second to enter was presented with the hind leg of an ox, the third with the fore leg. The honoured hero of the whole army was Mtusu, for he was the first to scramble over the palisade and drop into the town.

The chief, as he gave him the ox, derided the older men who had allowed a mere child to go before them, for Mtusu was still an unmarried lad and could not be counted a man.

The little lithe figure, whitened with clay, crowned with a tremendous head-dress of feathers and carrying a great shield and a spear from which the dried blood of victims was not yet washed, now dashed into the heart of the kraal and danced fiercely, leaping into the air and falling on his face before the great chief, while all the warriors rattled their shields and sang in chorus. Faster and wilder grew his dance, defiance blazed from his eyes, and the chief laughed at the youngster's enthusiasm and ordered further gifts for him. He was a lad to be marked. Such stuff as he was made of guaranteed a victorious race.

The quiet days in the mission house and school now seemed drab and uninteresting. Mtusu's soul was ablaze with ambition for war glory.

Chapter VII

RESTLESS DESIRES

MTUSU was now wedded to war. The hideous siren had kissed him and embraced him till passion had responded to passion. He had wet his spear in blood, and had not recoiled in loathing, for there was glory in it, and the kraal sang his praises. School was completely forgotten. The day was full of other interests, drinking, hunting, dancing, with occasional little raids involving two or three weeks' absence. As he was a blooded warrior he was admitted to the circle of the beer pot, and could sit for hours with the men drinking till he was full of song and fight.

He had won the right to marry. The story of his exploits made many a father seek him for a son-in-law, and many a high-born girl sent messengers to propose to him. For the warrior was the ideal husband for the free-born woman. His spear got many a slave, and, when there were domestic slaves to pound the maize and draw the water and hoe the gardens, the free-born wives had leisure to sit with those who gathered about the beer pot, and sometimes to brew gallons and gallons of sweet, heady beer.

Restless Desires

Besides, and chiefly, what virtue in man is more adorable in the eyes of woman, be she black or white, than courage and daring?

It was the modest right of young women to propose to an attractive man. They might begin the negotiations through some of their friends, and, if the young man responded, his friends carried through the treaty and arranged with the prospective father-in-law what number of cows should be paid over as dowry to him in exchange for his daughter.

But Mtusu had no thought of marriage. He believed it would hinder his success as a fighter and weaken his courage and strength. So offer after offer was rejected. There were heart-burnings over his indifference, and certain head-men felt grossly insulted that this lad should reject their offer of a most comely and eligible daughter. Again bitterness was increased, and men lay in wait to do him hurt for the insult he had put upon their village.

To the young men of Hoho, however, he was a great hero. They saw how he now despised the school and the gentle teaching of the mission, and they followed his example. He led their dances and their military exercises, and he showed them how to drink and to terrorise the people when his passions were inflamed.

Yet in the very days of his greatest military ardour the mission had begun subtly to direct the energies of the people in another direction. For it had come right into the heart of the Hoho villages and was opening a little sub-station. That meant the building of a school. Here were work and payment for all. Even the women and children found there was something for them to do, mud to tramp, grass to cut, and all was paid for in calico. Here was wealth at their

Restless Desires

very doors, far more tangible and certain than the spoils of raiding, and got without long and arduous expeditions.

Mtusu could not escape from the encompassing influence of the white man, and he became one of a gang of labourers who were sent forth to bring in trees for the building.

One afternoon he did not appear along with the other workers who were carrying their load of wood. Mr. Charles Stuart, who was looking after the building, missed him and asked where he was. Someone answered that he was resting in his village. Indeed that was his occupation, for when he had passed near his home in the forenoon he had heard the sound of a big carousal. He could not stop to join the merrymakers, but told them to see that some beer was reserved against his return.

At the midday rest he went to his village and began to enjoy the drink that had been kept for him. Now the conversation became very interesting, and, though the hour for resuming work had come, Mtusu sat lifting his beer pot for long, delicious draughts. When the pot was finished, in the joy of his soul he fetched his *gubu*,* and, joining the idlers on the ant-hill, sang his songs of war and triumph.

Meanwhile Mr. Stuart had set off for Mtusu's village to rout out the absentee, and there he saw our young friend seated on the ant-hill singing the passion of his soul to the accompaniment of the *gubu*.

Mr. Stuart interrupted the song very sharply, and called to Mtusu to come to him. Without any hesitation the songster laid down his instrument and descended unsteadily to the white man.

* A one-stringed musical instrument.

72

Restless Desires

" Why have you left your work, and why do you sit here idling ? " asked the master.

" I made two journeys and now am drinking," answered the unabashed foreman. " I sit here because the beer is here."

" Clear out ! " cried Mr. Stuart sternly. " There is no more work for you." This summary dismissal did not please Mtusu, and he followed Mr. Stuart, demanding his pay, and threatening him with an axe. When no notice was taken of his truculence, his pride, inflamed with beer, broke into a wild passion. Forgetting all his awe of the European, he dived into his hut, seized his spear and shield, and followed Mr. Stuart to the work-field. There he attacked him, determined to kill him for the insult. A struggle followed, and Mtusu was overpowered and fled back to his village.

When the effects of the beer had passed and sense returned Mtusu was so ashamed and afraid that he left his own village and buried himself in the royal village. There he stayed for four days till his mother came to fetch him back. Wiser counsels now prevailed, and he went to make his apologies to Mr. Stuart.

" Teacher," he said shamefacedly, " I have done you a great wrong. It was all because I was drunk." " Yes, you did wrong," answered his master. " Get back to your work." There the matter ended. Yet he could not forget, and years afterwards, when he was a leading Christian teacher, the memory of that episode made him squirm with shame.

Some time after this Mtusu was sitting alone in the lads' hut spending a lazy Saturday afternoon. Work was not so exciting as war, and in the quiet, unoccupied moments other voices could speak and be heard. He bethought himself of his Zulu Testament, which had lain neglected in a basket ever since the great raid when he had distinguished himself. From the basket he took out the book and read slowly and painfully. It was the Gospel of Mark he opened, for that was the simplest story, and he had often read it in school as a text-book. He began at the first chapter and had got as far as the fifteenth verse when he was suddenly arrested.

" The time is fulfilled, and the Kingdom of God is at hand. Repent ye, and believe the Gospel." He read again, wondering what mystery was in these words. He could easily understand the stern command to repent, and there were words there that seemed to point to an immediate urgency. What was it that was fulfilled ? What time had now come ? Perhaps there was something there that explained why the white men were so pressing.

He shut the book puzzled, and determined to probe the mystery.

Next day was Sunday. For a long time he had avoided the preaching at the station. It made him uncomfortable, and the word spoken there was not a message that agreed with his ambitions. But this morning he looked towards the station on the hill-side and saw that the white flag was flying to tell a calendarless people that this was the Lord's day. So he rose, and, crossing the Kasitu River, he climbed the hill to be there at the hour of worship. That day the missionary was preaching from the text, John x. 9 : " I am the door ; by Me if any man enter in he shall be saved." As he proceeded, Mtusu did not grasp any particular truth, but the impression came to him that here was a great thing, greater than anything in the world, and he must try and find out what this big thing was.

Restless Desires

Now Mtusu had reached the highest class in the ordinary school, that is to say he had learned to read the Bible in his own tongue in halting fashion. But there was an afternoon class carried on for the three or four monitors who helped to teach the lower classes, so he determined he would enter this class by becoming a monitor.

On Monday, without telling any of his companions, he went to the missionary and said, " I want to teach in the school." " All right. Go to your own village school at Chinyera and help there," he answered.

Then began Mtusu's career as a servant of the mission. He knew he had nothing to give, but he hoped that somehow he would be put in the way of further knowledge.

His work lasted only for little over an hour in the morning, but he heard the missionary give the Bible lesson each day and lead the prayers of those who frequented the little school. All day he worked about the mission ground glad to be employed in any work that was going, and greedy for anything he could pick up that revealed to him the mystery he sought to penetrate.

His new absorption did not pass unnoticed by the other men. He no longer sat idly with them, or joined in any of the raids that still took place.

" Why is it that when there is so much fighting we no longer see you ? " they cried. " Have you become a slave of the white man ? "

But Mtusu only sat silent with shame, for he did not understand himself, or the strong attraction the mission had for him. When the regiments gathered, the old spirit rose wildly in him, and he would join them. But always he found himself making for the mission station in the morning. His example was not lost on his fellows, who moved with the chief's son as a loyal company, and sought to do as he did.

Other villagers and head-men grew angrier and more jealous of the Hoho prepossession for the Europeans and their teaching. A disease had been introduced among the tribe, they thought, which was destroying its unity and power. Some of them would be glad to extirpate the disease by killing the Europeans and their followers.

Once in the earlier days of the mission Mtusu took his gun and went to hunt ducks on the Kasitu pools. He had a grand morning's sport and shot ten wild ducks. Then he cleaned his gun, and, carrying his bag, he started back for his village, passing near the head village of the great *induna* Chivukutu (" bellows "). Just as he approached the outskirts of the town he heard the war-herald crying from an ant-hill, " *Muyezwa-na ?* Why are you sitting still ? Maheyu has died at Hoho."

Now Maheyu was one of Chivukutu's people, and here was good excuse for attacking Hoho. Immediately the village started into activity like a nest of disturbed ants. Men ran for their spears and shields, and Mtusu could hear some shouting, " Let us make for Chinyera and kill the people there, together with the white men ! " This was no time for loitering, so he threw his birds aside and raced with all speed for his own village to warn the people that they would be attacked. In a moment all was bustle and fear. The women fled to the hills that they might be safe when the fight began. The men tore up the ant-hills and stood there armed, waiting for the coming of their enemies.

By and by they spied the warriors winding through

the bush in full battle array. They took their way towards the mission house, and it seemed as if nothing would save the defenceless Europeans from the long-suppressed hatred of these men. Suddenly the Hoho people saw the armed party cluster together in great agitation, and then finally break and run for their lives, some in their terror throwing aside shields and spears.

The whole affair was a mystery to the watchers. They could see no opposing army, no cause of the sudden panic and flight. Afterwards they learned that as the war-party wound their way towards the mission the sun had struck upon the windows of the Europeans' house. Great sheets of flaming water seemed to burst from the house. Horrified at the strange magic, which was only the sun's reflection on glass, but was new and terrifying to the ignorant savages, they fled for their lives, fearing that the wizard power of the European would follow and pierce them.

Again and again, however, the people showed their hatred of the Hoho folk who had been bewitched by the Europeans. Stragglers of Hoho parties who might be making a journey were waylaid and brutally attacked for no other reason than that their clan was friendly to the mission. Hoho was accused of having invited the Europeans into the country, and now of harbouring them when all the tribe would gladly see them cleared out.

"You could have killed them when you first met them," men growled. "But now they have settled among us, and are constantly teaching that we must give up raiding. They are bringing us all to poverty. Our wives are broken down with the hard work of drawing water and fetching firewood. We no longer can recruit our villages with slaves carried back in war."

So the Hoho people became isolated from the rest of the tribe and were hated more than any other section. But theirs was not the gift of reconciling enemies, and their boastfulness and flaunted wealth, gathered by work for the Europeans, only increased the bad feeling against them.

Chapter VIII

DISCUSSIONS

BY THE AUTHOR ON THE IMPORTANCE OF LITTLE THINGS ;
ALSO BETWEEN OUR HERO AND IMPULSIVE DAVID
ON THE NEW DOCTRINES TAUGHT AND ON THE
MYSTERY OF PAYMENT FOR TEACHING

YEARS of patient work were passing over the little band of Europeans who had claimed the Abangoni for Christ, but none had yielded to Him. Some few were learning to read and write, and many others knew now that work brings more pay than war. Yet no change appeared in the current of tribal life. After eight years not a soul had discovered the power of Christ's Gospel. At length two lads, sons of the great witch-doctor, professed their faith. Through all the years they had stuck by the mission in spite of severe persecution. Often in peril of their lives they had come to the missionary secretly in the dark to learn what he could teach them. Both of these lads were friends of Mtusu and belonged to the Hoho group of villages.

Yet, though results were so few and the price paid for these seemed out of all proportion, no sense of failure depressed the staff. Already two missionaries had died. Perpetual fevers and alarms, much physical discomfort and a great isolation were the conditions of evangelism. The petty service that cultured and educated men were giving seemed trivial and remote

from the purposes they had in view. But each minute
act was a preparation of the foundations for the temple
which was yet to be built. The superficial onlooker
might ask what was the use of all this trouble to teach
savages to do a little work. But the missionary knew
that every rebuke for indolence or slovenly work, and
every example of diligent faithfulness, were giving
lessons in honesty and justice, awakening slowly new
intelligence without which no ethical structure could
be raised. Hours were spent teaching the alphabet
and primer to pupils who were irregular in their
attendance and slow to make progress. But all the
while some were being introduced to the knowledge
that would make the Bible a speaking book, and a
few were unconsciously being prepared to be assistant
heralds of the Gospel. The Europeans were well
aware that they must train others to work for their
own countrymen, and that Africa's future depended
not on flooding the continent with foreign teachers,
but on creating native servants of the people.

This young savage who was told to lay out a line
of bricks in a row laid them in a curve, for a straight
line was foreign to him. Day by day he was taught
and corrected until at last he laid something resembling
a straight line, and the missionary knew that here
was an embryo builder who one day would be able
to follow the line and plumb a wall till a good house
stood which would be safe to live in.

This lad, clad in two yards of calico, who was teaching the alphabet, without science and in most blunder-
ing way, might some day become a trained teacher
learned in the methods of pedagogy and lead his
people into fuller knowledge.

These men and women, naked but for their little
monkey skins or strips of bark cloth, who listened

Discussions

day by day at sunrise to a gospel story and learned a simple hymn and heard the missionary pray, would some day see the little light shining by the wicket gate and would enter in to the wonders of a life of fellowship with God. This was the greatest and most essential service. For these missionaries believed that in the Christian Gospel there is a dynamic which creates new characters, rebuilds a nation and brings in the Kingdom of God.

In the little school at Chinyera the young heathen warrior Mtusu could be seen day by day teaching a crowd of lads and girls to identify those mystic signs which we call the alphabet. He knew little of the Christian way, but he was hungry to find out where it lay. Meanwhile he gave what knowledge he had to his more ignorant fellows, and that scarcely exceeded the knowledge of the first elements of reading. But every afternoon he and another lad, David, climbed up the scarred, bush-covered path that led to Njuyu mission station and there received further instruction from the white man. Sometimes great discussions took place over the things they heard, but all their talk only led them into a deeper maze.

One day they had a great dispute about the sermon they had heard on the Sabbath. Little did the European preacher think that his simple words had left so cloudy an impression, for he had been speaking on the death of Christ.

David explained : " This man Jesus, whom the European spoke about as dying, died for the white man."

Mtusu cried : " You lie there ! That is not how it is. Jesus is the Son of God. God sent His Son into the world to die for the white man. They came to tell us the words they had received from God. And

Discussions

when Mtusane (William Koyi) died, he was a black man and he died for us Abangoni, that we might worship our Mtusane and not the spirit of the great chief who led the tribe. Mtusane will bring our message to Jesus, and Jesus will tell it to God, His Father."

The dispute grew hot, and at last they both cried, " Let us go to the white man and ask him ! " So they went to the missionary and told him of their discussion. He was immensely interested, and said to them :

" You are both wrong. Mtusane was only a man, and he had no such authority as you think he had. But Jesus is God, and He died for white and black alike."

Then Dr. Elmslie's text from John x. 9 came whispering back to Mtusu's memory, and he went home saying to himself, " Does He ask that I should come to His door ? He must be very gracious if He thinks of us black people. May I come to His door ? Oh that I could see Him ! "

When Mtusu had been teaching for some time he was called up to Njuyu along with his friend, David, and each received six yards of calico. Now David was a serf of Mtusu's family and was devoted most loyally to his young master. He was a hot-headed, passionate youth who never turned his other cheek to the smiter, but rather seized his knobkerrie and gave back better than he got. But as he had followed Mtusu in war, he now followed him in learning, and was ready to endure anything for his loyalty. Years afterwards his undisciplined character led him into many an ugly scrape while he was still in the mission service, but he came laughing out of the biggest mess.

Discussions

Towards the end of his life he was imprisoned by a European native commissioner in Northern Rhodesia for having smashed the beer pots of some villagers who were drinking on a Sabbath day. He thought he was following the way of Jesus in the Temple with those who sold and bought there, and he rejoiced in the violence of his indignation. But the villagers were equally indignant and complained to the magistrate, who saw only danger in such methods of reformation. For some time David lay in prison in chains, until the magistrate fell seriously ill, and started off for the nearest European settlement, taking his prisoners with him, but he died before he reached it. On the way his sickness did not allow him to guard his prisoners too carefully, so one night David slipped off. By night he travelled towards home, for he had been pioneering in a distant tribe. By day he hid in the bush. And so he travelled secretly, suffering greatly from hunger. When at last he arrived at my station he was so thin and starved that he had slipped off the handcuffs over his emaciated hands. With a laugh he gave the irons into my charge and went on his way to his own people, after telling me his story. Of course I had to express my stern disapproval of my hot-headed reformer. To this day the handcuffs hang in my office, for the succeeding commissioners would not take them back as there was no inventory of them in their office. They hang there to remind me of my old zealous friend who has long ago crossed the River.

But I have greatly overstepped the bounds of history. For we left Mtusu and David, his friend, each rich in the possession of six yards of calico which they had received for their first service in the mission school. They had no thought of payment, for they both served

Discussions

so that they might have the privilege of being taught again by the European in the afternoon.

Silently and greatly puzzled they wended their way home. At length David stopped and said, " Let us sit down and spread out our cloth that we may see it."

So they sat down by the wayside and spread out the cloth. What endless reaches of calico were there, clean, fresh, untorn ! What were they to do with it ?

" See now," said David, " the white man has given us all this cloth. We have not bought it. We brought nothing with us which we might have given in exchange. Does the white man want to get us into a quarrel with him by giving us what is not ours ? Let us show it to our elders that they may know we are in disgrace with our master, seeing we are in possession of this cloth. Perhaps they will redeem us and give us cattle to pay for the cloth."

" No, no ! " cried Mtusu, " If that is how the case stands, let us return to the teacher and give him back his cloth. I don't want to be in disgrace because I have calico which I did not buy. He gave it to us. We did not steal it."

But this suggestion alarmed his friend, who was still in dread of the incomprehensible white man and all his queer ways.

" Don't let us go back with the cloth ! " he cried. " It is dangerous to bother the white man. Down at the Lake I once saw a man go up to speak to a European, and he set his dog on him to bite him. Just let us keep quiet. We won't tear up the cloth, only let our elders see it."

So home they went, and handed over the mysterious and troublesome calico to their parents that they might keep it safely.

84

Discussions

Next day, when Mtusu went up to Njuyu for his afternoon lessons, he ventured to unburden himself to Mr. Scott. " Why did you give us the cloth ? " he asked. " Do you wish us to buy sheep and goats with it and bring them to you ? "

" What cloth ? " asked the teacher, puzzled. " When did I give it to you ? "

" Yesterday," answered Mtusu. " You gave us six yards of calico each."

Then Mr. Scott went into roars of laughter, and at last cried, " No, no ! my child. The calico is yours. You have been helping us to teach the children in school. That is your pay."

Then it dawned on Mtusu that teaching also was work deserving pay, and he went out and solemnly explained the matter to the others. But still it was all too wonderful, and for four months those six yards lay in the safe keeping of his mother. He could not summon courage to divide them, and still feared that a mistake had been made and this great treasure would be demanded back.

Chapter IX

THE DECISION

FOLLOWS AN INSISTENT DREAM AND THE HEALING
TOUCH OF GOD ON MTUSU'S CHILD

ALTHOUGH Mtusu had identified himself with
the mission he had by no means accepted
either its standard of ethics or its faith. He
was still an ignorant heathen with some realisation
that great truths were hidden from him which were
worth finding.

In 1892 he finally left the hut where the young
men lived together, and, having built a house for
himself, took to wife Tungeya, the daughter of
Maumba, a neighbouring head-man, to whom he paid
many cattle as dowry. But no free-born woman
would consent to have the whole drudgery and
labour of caring for a husband laid upon her shoulders
alone. She expected that other wives would share
her responsibility, though each would necessarily
have a hut of her own and serving-women to attend
on her. So Mtusu responded to the offers of other
girls and entered into negotiations with their fathers
for marriage with them at some future time. Fathers
and daughters were ready to consent to marriage
with one who had so distinguished himself in
war.

While he was a table-boy Mtusu had the advantage
of seeing day by day how a Christian gentleman

The Decision

behaves to his wife, yet it must not be assumed that he made any effort to imitate this in his own life. The white people were not of the same order of human beings, and what was right and proper for them might be altogether wrong and improper for the Abangoni.

Thus he never ate along with his young wife. She would have keenly resented such a suggestion, for women are the greatest guardians of custom and taboo. Each evening a dish of white maize porridge with a little pot of relish was carried out to the kraal gate where he sat with the other men, and laid at his feet on the ground. Four or five of his intimate friends were invited to eat, and, sitting down on their haunches after washing their hands, they surrounded the food and ate with their fingers. Later on the wife of another member of the group would appear with his dish of food, and all would eat together from this fresh supply until they were satisfied.

The greater part of the day was spent by Tungeya in the society of other village women, and she seldom spoke to her husband till the evening came and they were alone in their own hut. Too often beer was freely drunk, and then very slight differences would burst into serious quarrels. Mtusu had the native belief that a wife is made to serve the husband, and that the best results are got by the man's showing himself physically the stronger. Blows were better teachers than kisses.

Yet his mind was not easy. He had often heard that polygamy was wrong, and that a gentler monogamy was the Christian ideal, but he did not like this way, neither did his wife.

One night he dreamed that someone spoke to him and said, " Mtusu, how many wives have you ? "

The Decision

He answered, " I have five girls betrothed to me, and one wife who is with me."

Then the voice said sternly, " Stop ! "

A second time he heard the words, " Mtusu, how many wives have you ? "

" Five, and the wife who is with me," he answered again. " Stop ! " said the voice.

Six times that night the voice seemed to ask him, and when he had answered the same stern reply came, " Stop ! "

Now dreams have a large influence on the minds of the people, for then it is that the spirits speak. So in the morning Mtusu told his wife of his experience. He was so serious about it that she was quick enough to divine that he was thinking of listening to this voice, and she sharply told him that if he gave up those betrothed girls she would leave him and return to her father's village. She did not wish to cook and sweep alone. He argued with her, but she absolutely refused to stay with him if she were to be sole wife. To all the reasons that he could bring she answered with a decided " No ! I refuse to stay."

This was very upsetting. Evidently it was not going to be too easy to obey what he believed was a heavenly vision, and there was no one in his village who could help him or who saw eye to eye with him. However, he wrote a note to Mawelera, the first native to be a Christian, a man of peculiarly attractive character and of no small influence, and asked him to come across and talk to his wife. Mawelera eagerly came and did his best to instruct Tungeya, but all through the conversation she continued her refrain, " I shall go back to my home if Mtusu gives up those girls."

The Decision

Mtusu was greatly depressed by this failure to carry his wife with him. Then the words of Matthew's Gospel came to him that a man's foes shall be those of his own household. Day by day the emphatic word of the vision, "Stop!" rang in his ears, and he knew that he must obey it. So he decided to wait to see whether his wife would not change her intention. The village elders, however, soon heard of the difficulty between him and his wife. They were indignant that this son of Chipatula should forsake the ways of his fathers, and they saw much discomfort for themselves and their daughters should such mad customs be followed in their tribe. Under this fear they confirmed the opposition of Tungeya, and stiffened her resolution to go back to her father's house were Mtusu to refuse those to whom he was betrothed.

Now at this time their one little boy, then scarcely more than a year old, became seriously ill. Day by day the fever continued and would yield to no treatment. Little magical sticks were tied about his forehead and on his body, but they could not turn away the sickness. His skin was scarified and a black, oily medicine was rubbed into the wounds, yet the fever only increased. The doctor was called. He prepared his vile concoctions and poured them down the boy's throat; he beat his drum and danced in wild array, but the evil spirit which had entered the child refused to yield possession.

Utterly beaten and greatly distressed, the parents waited to see their only son die. One evening they sat beside him, while Mtusu read and re-read Luke vii. 1–10, and thought how Jesus healed the sick in His pity when He was on earth. How he wished He was here to do it now! Yet had he not heard again

The Decision

and again that Jesus was still alive and able to save? He doubted and feared, wondering if He would hear if he prayed. At length, when they were utterly broken with the constant cries of the little boy, he said to his wife, " The child will die, but let me try to pray." She agreed that he might do so if he wished, but she refused to listen to his prayer.

Then he knelt and prayed, " Jesus, if You healed the child of the centurion, and if You are the maker of everything, as the teacher says, save my child quickly. If You will save the boy I will be Your slave, my wife will be Your slave, and the boy will be Your slave. And so my wife and I will have one mind, and I will renounce those to whom I am betrothed. Amen."

When the prayer was over the parents sat down quietly and waited. They were both very tired and by and by fell into deep sleep. As the cold dawn began to break Mtusu seemed to dream, and then wakened suddenly. He remembered his little sick boy, and wept to think that the child must have died while he slept. The mother was still sleeping soundly, and he leaned over to look on his dead child, but was amazed to see that he was in a deep sweat, the perspiration was running on to the mat, and he was breathing quietly. The father took him up in his arms, but did not waken his wife or wait to blow up the fire.

Then the mother wakened and cried, " Is the child dead? Is he dead? "

" Take the child," said Mtusu ; " he is alive and well. The water on the mat is his sweat."

Tungeya wept as she took her little boy to her breast, and asked her husband to blow up the fire so that they might see. Then they were able to look

The Decision

on their son and be assured that he was well, and they gave him milk, which he drank readily.

Mtusu sat very quietly on the mat looking with great tenderness on his wife, but saying nothing. After a while she broke the silence, saying :

" I greatly erred about that dream of yours. See, the child has recovered because of your prayer. I shall stay with you though you give up all the girls to whom you are betrothed. Should my father and mother come to confirm me in my old refusal I shall answer them nothing. Serve God along with me."

With a tremendous joy in his heart Mtusu knelt again and prayed, " O God, at last I know You, and I am Your slave. I swear I will not leave You. Help me till I rest in my grave. My wife is Yours too. And my child is Yours. Keep him till he grows to know You and is Your slave. You have shown Yourself to me, the worst of all men. I will be Your slave for ever."

That morning Mtusu climbed the hill to the mission station and made his confession to Dr. Steele, who was now settled there, for Dr. Elmslie had passed on to open a new station at Ekwendeni. He told him the whole story of his wife, and all about the sickness of the child, and how God had come to them. Dr. Steele listened quietly to the tale, making no comment. When Mtusu had finished, the doctor sat still, looking like a man before whom heaven has opened. Then suddenly he said :

" Let us pray. Ah, no ! Mtusu, you will pray ! "

Then Mtusu prayed, with a great peace in his heart, and the words came, for joy and thankfulness were flowing like a full stream. When he finished, the doctor only added a word or two, for he said :

The Decision

"Father, Thou revealest Thyself by many ways. Thy paths we cannot count, but they lead to Thee. Be with Mtusu all the time, and with his wife, and with the child. Amen."

Now the marriage of the other girls with Mtusu had been arranged with the parents, and soon they were all to be sent on to him. So the young convert asked Dr. Steele to help him in his difficult negotiations with the parents when he would tell them that he no longer desired to have their daughters.

But Steele was not at all sure what was the right thing to do. So far the missionaries had not dealt with the problem of polygamists becoming Christian, and there were many reasons why a man should fulfil his responsibility to those whom he had taken to be his wives, and not cast them adrift. On the other hand, there were no dangers before these rejected women, for they could marry again, or if they preferred could live single in the village of their parents and relatives, who would care for them. But the most serious question was the social morality of the Church that was to be. If polygamy was countenanced in any form the Church could not stand for that ideal home life which must be the foundation of Christian society.

At this time a clear decision had not been made, and the missionaries were not yet intimately acquainted with the customs and thought of the people. So Dr. Steele doubted very much whether Mtusu should not marry the girls he had betrothed. But there was no doubt or hesitation in Mtusu's mind as he said with emphasis :

"No ! no ! All night I struggled with this question, 'How many wives have you ? ' I have promised God, and I cannot go back."

The Decision

"Well," said Steele, "there is to be a meeting of missionaries at Ekwendeni presently. Dr. Laws and Dr. Elmslie are to be there. I shall speak with them, and if they say that you should leave these girls, I shall write to you at once. But if they advise otherwise you will also obey."

So the question was kept open, and Mtusu returned to his village. Four days after Dr. Steele wrote to Mtusu to tell him that all the missionaries were agreed that he should do as he intended and renounce the girls to whom he was betrothed.

Here let me interpolate that experience has fully confirmed the wisdom of this decision, and all missions in Nyasaland make it a rule that no polygamist can be received into the Church until he has renounced all his wives except the first one he married, for she alone is the true wife.

As soon as Mtusu heard this decision he sent off messengers to the parents of his betrothed and told them that he no longer desired to marry their daughters. No serious objection was urged by the fathers, for no dowry cattle had yet been paid. But with the girls the message was not quietly received. They had chosen him, as was their right, and they were not prepared to give up so attractive a husband without protest. So the girls themselves came to the village to speak with Mtusu. They asked whether the word which the messengers had carried was true and whether he had finally renounced them all.

"Yes," said Mtusu, "it is true. Go away and marry other husbands. But as for me, I must be the husband of one wife only."

That was a difficult day for the poor man, for the girls pressed their desire for him, urged him with soft entreaties, then with mockery, and finally with

93

The Decision

bitterness. But as he remained obdurate, they left, weeping, amid painful scenes.

It was not long before they all had given themselves to other husbands for good or for ill. But the memory of the insult that Mtusu had put on them and their villages was the source of dangerous persecution in coming days, and the men who had looked for an honourable alliance with Mtusu and his family through sisters and daughters now sought for cause of quarrels and fighting by which they might do him hurt.

Chapter X

THE BAPTISM

IS DESCRIBED, AND THE WONDERFUL MYSTIC VISION THAT DANIEL SAW

IT was in the midst of the rainy season, and the people were busy in their gardens hoeing down the weeds and heaping the earth about the roots of the growing maize. No villager cared to work alone. There was so much more cheerfulness in a crowd, and the work was done more rapidly. Great quantities of beer were brewed by the housewives, and, when the fermentation was complete, word was sent out that on the morrow such and such a garden would be hoed. At early dawn men and women assembled at the field with their hoes, and after a little drinking the work began. The valley rang with their shouts and song, and a great impression of hard, joyful labour was given. But every now and then a tired hoer laid down his implement and joined the group about the beer pots. As the day proceeded the noise increased, but the real work decreased, and by evening the field was finished in some fashion and the workers returned to their homes. They wended their way shouting their drunken songs, or tumbled about in the path, and sat down at times to recover themselves. In the evening the villages were noisy and full of the dance of the excited workers, or too often were scenes of wild

The Baptism

pandemonium and fighting, when quarrelsome drunkards hit at one another with clubs that threatened sore damage.

The 5th of February, 1895, was a Sunday, and the big white flag was flying at the mission station to proclaim the day. To most it had no interest, and for many the knowledge that beer was ready for other fields was far more attractive. But this was no common day, for it was reported that several men and women were to receive the magic water of baptism and this day were to be made Christians. So the people poured into the station from many villages. They sat about in groups, carrying on endless chatter about all kinds of things save those connected with religion and worship.

By and by the little bell was rung and they flowed into the simple building that served both as church and school. They were all dirty, naked people, and what little calico was worn was soiled with rain and earth. Some of the men wearing the round Zulu head-ring pushed their way through the crowd which squatted on the floor and murmured something about *amajaha* and *amadoda*, which everyone knew to mean that boys should give place to grown men. They took their place in front, near the platform, laying down their clubs with a clatter on the floor. Four or five dogs wandered after them, picking their way among the projecting knees and receiving now and then a vigorous thump on the ribs from some lad, which made them yelp, but scarcely hastened their movement. Back towards the door a crowd of women and girls were seated in a thick mass. Every woman seemed to have a baby tied to her back in a goat's skin, and not a few of the babies were already squalling vigorously. Outside the low open windows

MILKING A COW

The hind legs are tethered, and the calf stands beside the mother. Without this the
herd would get no milk.

A PATIENT FOR THE HOSPITAL

The Baptism

little boys were standing looking in, while others ran about with much shouting, all of which was as audible to the congregation as if they played within the building.

On a form beside the platform were seated the only intelligent and responsive part of the congregation. There were the two sons of the witch-doctor who had already been baptized. Beside them sat the six men and two women who were now to be received into the fellowship of the Church. Mtusu was there, his copper skin polished to shining with soap and water, and about his body a few yards of clean, new calico. At his feet his wife was seated with the little boy, brought back from the dead, lying quietly in her lap.

Among the others were Mtusu's young brother, Yobe, his friends Andrew and Hezekiah, both of whom will one day be ordained ministers of the Church into which they now enter through the waters of baptism. The women were the wives of the first converts.

By and by, while the children were still squalling and the dogs snarling at one another, a little European dressed in white duck and followed by one or two other missionaries advanced through the crowd, picking his way carefully that he might not tread on anyone. This was Dr. Steele, the devoted physician, who was winning a great place for himself in the affections of the people. He seated himself in a high chair—much too high for his little legs—and laid his books on the white cloth of the table, on which also stood a baptismal vessel.

After the missionary had engaged in a short silent prayer the worship began with the singing of a very simple hymn in which quite a few were able to join.

G 97

The Baptism

Then followed a long prayer, and then more singing, the reading of the scriptures and of the commandments. After this a sermon was preached in Chingoni, but only a few could follow the address, given as it was in a wooden, foreign way, and dealing with things that were new to the people.

The whole service had little in it that would have impressed the European stranger or the massed, ignorant heathen. But to some it was the most memorable service of their life, for they sat there, waiting for the gate to be opened which would admit them to the fellowship of the Catholic Church of Jesus Christ.

At last the moment came. Standing before the crowd of their fellows, Mtusu and the other converts answered firmly the questions that were put to them concerning their faith. Then the little doctor baptized them in the name of the Father, Son and Holy Ghost, giving to Mtusu the new name Daniel. The congregation dispersed slowly to their distant villages, but ten Christians remained behind, and that afternoon, in company with their missionaries, partook of the Holy Communion of the body and blood of Christ.

When all was over, Daniel Mtusu Nhlane returned to his village in a state of great exaltation, He was ever a mercurial man, and this day the thermometer was at its highest possible register. With his soul ablaze for the glory that had come to him in being admitted a full member of the Church of Christ he entered his hut and began to read the Gospel of St. John. He was still reading, when lo! a vision appeared. He was not asleep : his eyes were wide open, and a Person stood before him. He needed not to speak. Amid ten thousand times ten

The Baptism

thousand he would have known Him, and in the tumult of a universe he would have recognised His voice.

For He spoke, saying, " I am He in Whom you have believed. You need not ask. See, I am He Whom you covenanted to serve."

He knew that he was in the room with the living Jesus, and he cried out that He should not leave him. A great light seemed to fill the dark hut, and in his joy he began to sing the hymn " Come to Jesus just now." Again he read his Bible, and it spoke to him till his soul gloried in the excellency of Christ.

Then he called to his brothers that they might come and see how wonderful was the Saviour who had found him. He spoke with a joy and conviction that were irresistible, and these men, who had watched with great displeasure the turn that Mtusu had taken, went away with most serious thoughts. Not many days passed till all three decided that they, too, must follow in the Way. One of them was a polygamist, but he put away his other wives, only retaining his first one. Soon afterwards they also were received into the Christian Church, and all three became mission teachers. Others, too, in the village were deeply moved and began to seek instruction, and made their confession of faith.

But the old people in the village were not pleased, and they said that Daniel was leading many astray. They counted him worse than a murderer, for he had been disloyal to all the history and traditions of the people. Yet for him and his fellow-seekers there was nothing but peace.

" Our hearts," he afterwards wrote, " drew near to the gate of the knowledge of the sweetness of the

The Baptism

Gospel. And there is nothing in the world that beats the sweetness of it."

Now he understood the meaning of Dr. Elmslie's words in the old days, that if he continued to learn he would receive good and sweet things.

Chapter XI

THE WITNESS

OF DANIEL'S CONDUCT CHANGES SOME AND
PUZZLES OTHERS

DANIEL MTUSU continued to be a man of strong emotions. If sometimes he could rise to heights of ecstatic joy and fervour, there were other times, happily not frequent, when he was sullen and depressed. The emotion, however, which gripped him on the day of his baptism was no sudden and evanescent feeling. It was the culmination of months of desiring and seeking. There never entered into his mind a doubt that Jesus had actually come to him, was seen with his eyes and spoke audible words. Again and again through the years of his discipleship he had his days of great spiritual elation, and these moods deeply affected his character and service.

His friends all knew that he was a changed man. Not that he lost entirely the passions of the past. There were times when dangerous rumblings threatened volcanic eruptions, but they soon passed, for a new Power was now in control. The irrepressible energy and activity which found expression in war and cruel deeds now found in the service of the Kingdom of God a happier and more useful vent, leading him into most adventurous service. The passion which had made

him a terror gave place to a tenderness and courtesy
inventive of deeds of kindly solicitude.

To none was this sweetening of character more
evident than to his own wife. In his unregenerate
days he had used her as a masterful Mungoni should.
When she did not please him, blows bent her spirit
and proved that he was master in his own household.
She was only a woman after all, and not fit company
for a man who delighted in war and scorned the
softness that came to those too devoted to the
luxuries of village life. Daniel's new attitude to
Christ altered his attitude to everything else. His
loyalty to his own family only deepened, and made
him seek first his brothers that they might rejoice
with him in his Saviour. The hut in which he slept
now became a home, and his wife a companion. His
harshness to her was changed to a winsome thought-
fulness which would make her a sharer of the rich
life which was flowing all about him. This was all
so pleasant that Tungeya no longer resented his decision to follow the Christian rule of family life, but
herself became a disciple.

One day, when she sat with the other village women,
she made her confession to them in these words :

" Now I believe in God and in His wonderful
power, for He has changed my husband. You all
saw how he used to beat me every day and how he
had little but fierce words for me. I went about
with tears in my eyes, and I knew that the time was
coming when he and I must part, for we could not
live together in such hatred. To-day there is peace
in my house, and he often sits with me and talks
gently to me."

To such a testimony all could agree. For there is
nothing secret or private in village life. Every

quarrel between husband and wife can be heard through the thin walls of the hut. Too often the morning's disagreeableness uttered in the most foul language is shouted from the various huts. When the tempers rise, and with them the velocity of the tongues, a curious quiet falls upon the village, so that the little groups sitting outside around the fires, as well as the inmates of the various houses, hear all that is said. The children who grow up in such an environment have other educators than their own parents, and their childhood's innocence is early tarnished with the atmosphere around them.

Tungeya's witness to the change in her husband's conduct only confirmed what everyone knew, and many another woman wistfully looked for the day when her lot, too, would be sweetened by the same kind of conversion.

But to none was the new Mtusu more strange than to his own mother. She had nurtured him from his infancy, had seen his wild passions and knew how terrible he could be. Yet she had rejoiced in his reputation for bravery, and in the whispered tales of his cruelties and fightings. For neither she nor any other woman in the tribe recognised meekness and gentleness as virtues. Of such stuff a race of warriors is not made. Through all his wildest days he had retained the peculiar love and reverence for his mother, which is one of the attractive features of the Abangoni. Yet there was something in his attitude now more desirable than the passion she had admired. And when he spoke to her of his great discovery she, too, found herself strangely prejudiced in favour of his message and listened as one who would fain be a disciple.

All the villagers, however, were not so sympathetic.

The Witness

Some indeed were pleased, and as the Central African moves in groups, not a few of the young men cast in their lot with their leader and became pupils in the school and regular worshippers on the Sabbath. But others were indignant. They thought that the spirit of the tribe had been betrayed by the young convert, and declared that the missionaries had given him a potent medicine to break his manhood and that of the other lads.

What puzzled them most was the young men's indifference to women. "How can they live with only one wife?" they asked. "She will soon grow old, and then whom will the husband love, and who will care for his needs?" They foresaw the day when those who would not marry other women must gratify their passions in a lawless fashion. Then the villages would be ruined by their looseness. Fiercest of all was the opposition among those whose daughters Daniel had rejected. One attempt on his life was made for this insult, and for long afterwards he and his fellow-villagers were threatened and in frequent danger.

Determined efforts were also made to drag him into polygamy. It is a custom in the tribe for the father of the bride to honour his son-in-law and to express his delight in his fame or conduct by sending him another daughter to be a companion wife to her sister. This compliment was paid Daniel in all good faith by his father-in-law. It was one of those discords between conduct and faith which revealed a ridiculous misconception of our aims, as when a neighbouring head-man pushed his way through the crowd up to the platform where the missionary was preaching temperance and righteousness and laid at his feet a great gourd of intoxicating beer for his

refreshment; or when, some years later, the uncle
of the new paramount chief, on the day of his instal-
lation, prayed to Mombera's spirit that he might
" bless the teachers who went up and down the country
speaking the words of God."

So Daniel's parents-in-law, pleased with his kindness to his wife, sent him a younger sister in recognition, adding that they expected from him no
dowry for her. But Daniel returned her with a stern
word, saying:

" You are children of darkness. Why have I re-
frained from polygamy? Did I find evil in the girls
to whom I was betrothed and whom I rejected?
You seek to turn me from God, Who is better than
all the women in the world and all the riches that
can be given me."

For the ignorant and well-meaning parents Daniel
had no soft words of remonstrance. He spoke like
one defying wilful tempters, and they shrank back,
afraid and ashamed of their action, but not under-
standing. The news of this strange dealing with a
most handsome offer created some consternation in
the villages. Mothers wept for the hard lot that was
awaiting their daughters. When the Christian in-
fection spread over the land, where were husbands
to be found for eligible girls? There would be too
many women in the land if all men were only to
have one wife. In pagan Africa there are no unmarried women. " An old maid is a Christian institution." The fathers, who had counted every
daughter as banked money, looking to the day when
men would pay the usual dowry for them, were as
angry as shareholders would be over the action of
fraudulent directors. What right had Mtusu to rob
them of their invested wealth? For every daughter

The Witness

born there had been a special welcome, because she would increase the possessions of her parents by her marriage. Now the girls were to be on their hands, consuming food and bringing in nothing. So the men cried angrily that the missionaries had bewitched Mtusu and all his kind and were enemies of the people. Threats and violence were tried to turn Mtusu from the narrow way of monogamy, but without avail.

Chapter XII

A SHAMEFUL ASSAULT

IS MADE ON DANIEL BY LAWLESS MEN WHO RESENT HIS
LIFE AND DOCTRINE

ABOUT the time of Daniel's baptism the
Abangoni were without a supreme head.
The great chief was dead, and as his head
wife had no sons there was a disputed succession.
The councillors could not agree that any one of his
sons or brothers was the obvious heir, while the son
whom the father had on his death-bed named to be
his successor was a very indeterminate kind of lad
whose mother was not free born. The Hoho villages
also were still without a chief, for no one had been
appointed in Chipatula's place for very much the
same reasons.

The result was considerable lawlessness. Chiefs
and head-men quarrelled with one another and there
was no one to settle their disputes. Powerful men
took the law into their own hands and frequently
made life and property very unsafe by their violence.
The young sons of Mombera, unwhipped and undisciplined whelps, were constantly inciting to mischief
and leading lawless youths to prey on helpless serfs.

This gave opportunity for the enemies of Daniel
to threaten him, and he was in constant danger of
coming by serious harm. He was now teaching in
two schools, at Chinyera in the morning and at the

A Shameful Assault

village of his father-in-law Maumba in the afternoon.
This involved a walk of about three or four miles
each day. One evening when Daniel was on his way
home along with David, his companion teacher, he
met a man on the path who stopped him just for a
moment and warned him to be careful, for enemies
were plotting to kill him because he had taken up
customs which were different from those of the
country. As he turned to go away the stranger
said one word—" Beware ! "—and so passed on.

This serious warning depressed the two young men,
for they well knew that already two or three of their
fellow-villagers had been secretly killed for no other
reason but this disloyalty to the past.

David was as brave as any once his passions were
roused. Then his impetuous spirit knew no fear.
But it was another thing to hear this ominous
" Beware ! " in the bush, and in cold blood. Fear
almost paralysed his thought and action. Daniel,
however, was of much more reliable stuff, and rather
rejoiced when he scented adventure and danger.
Besides, his deep sense of God's companionship made
him very confident, so that he feared no one. Turning to his friend he said, " Let us kneel down here
and pray. God will deliver us so that no one can
harm us."

There by the path, enclosed by the thick scrub,
the two teachers commended themselves to God's
fatherly care.

As they rose to their feet again Daniel said to
erratic David, " Come along now. What does it
matter though danger threaten us ? God will protect us." In this confidence they both resumed their
journey.

They passed through Chiwazo's village and saw

there a son of the late great chief drinking along with a number of young men. This son was one of the most reactionary men in the tribe, headstrong, violent, unrestrained. He and his followers terrorised the helpless, demanding whatever they wanted, and threatening those who were unwilling to satisfy their demands. Frequently they attacked and burned villages of serfs within their own tribe, and no one could bring them to justice. The same rascal, however, was killed a year or so later during one of his robberies.

Daniel and his friend had just got beyond the confines of the village when they heard someone shouting after them, " Is it you who tell the people that they are not to become polygamists? You are ruining the chief's country ! "

Drunken passion was in the shout, while the din in the village revealed that the lawless young men were gathering to do mischief. The night was now falling, and the teachers were still some way from home. As soon as the noise of the hunt began, David took to his heels and fled through the thick bush, leaving Daniel to his fate. Soon the drunken men surrounded him, flourishing their clubs and shouting. Some cried, " Let us kill him ! " but others protested, saying, " No ! no ! let us thrash him soundly." So they beat him with their clubs until he was bruised all over. They thrust his mouth open and filled it with filth, and then threw him into the bush, where he lay stunned and unconscious.

The villagers thought he had been killed, and quickly the news flew to Njuyu. David, too, arrived there breathless with his flight and told how he had seen Daniel seized and threatened, and his story did not lose in the telling.

A Shameful Assault

Consternation and wild indignation burst out. The people at Hoho cried to one another to go forth and fight those brutal enemies. Quickly a little party, under the leadership of Mawelera, started out through the night. As they neared Chiwazo's village they met Daniel staggering home, and plied him with questions, until they knew the whole story of the assault. It was good to see their friend alive, but it was more necessary now that the upholders of peace should show that, if there was no chief in the land to restrain the lawless, they were strong enough to protect innocent travellers. In the quiet of the night, well hid by the thick bush land, they discussed their method of operations. It was agreed that they should surround the village, open the kraal gate and carry off all the cattle. Should they be attacked they would not use their spears but only their knob-kerries, and all should be careful to do no hurt to women or children.

Silently they spread themselves about the village, from which no light appeared, for it was now late and all the people were within their huts. Some of the party lifted the bars of the kraal gate and began to drive the cattle out. The beasts were unwilling to go, and the noise of their stampeding within the pen and of the drovers urging the beasts forth roused many of the villagers. In a few moments the whole place was astir, and men dashed out of the huts to protect their property. The Hoho lads had to fight to get the cattle off. Clubs whirling and beating against resounding shields, wild shouts and whistling gave all the impression of a fierce battle in the dark. But the Hoho men were careful never to strike at the head, but on the body only of the villagers who attacked them.

A Shameful Assault

At last the cattle were all out and were driven at a run through the bush, men surrounding them and keeping them going at a good pace, till they were safely shut within the kraal of one of the Hoho villages.

Next day Chiwazo's people went off to Mperembe, brother of the late paramount chief, who acted as a kind of regent for the tribe. He listened to their story, but was too practical a judge to make any decision after hearing one side only. Instead of calling all parties to his village court he sent some messengers to make inquiries into the whole business. When they returned and made their report it was very evident that the aggressors were Chiwazo's people and that they had been guilty of an unprovoked assault: so he ordered them to pay up to the village they had wronged.

The chief had spoken and had given a decision on their appeal, so there was nothing for it but to obey. Next day they arrived at Hoho with a cow and a goat as payment for the crime. But Daniel and his friends only accepted the goat. They returned the cow, together with the herd of cattle they had driven away, as they had no intention of making profit out of the incident, but only wished to let the men see that when they were attacked they were vigorous enough to defend themselves.

Chapter XIII

CITIZENSHIP

HAS MANY-SIDED DUTIES WHICH OUR HERO PERFORMS
NOT WITHOUT DANGER TO HIMSELF

IF the Abangoni were suffering a little from the lack of a strong central government, their neighbours reaped some advantages, for the great national raids ceased, though not through any definite intention on the part of the councillors, some of whom called constantly for a united expedition and were loud in their denunciation of the lethargy that was creeping over the tribe. By 1895 two of the chief rulers were dead, and the *indunas* disputed and delayed over the appointment of their successors. Meanwhile, just because there was no unifying authority, the raiding ambitions of the most ardent reactionaries failed to come to fruition. Every year, however, independent little marauding parties still harried the neighbouring tribes, but never in such strength as to be able to assert the old invincibility of the Abangoni.

Besides, the Europeans were increasing in numbers and authority. There was a strong mission station at Bandawe. Traders and missionaries were settled at Karonga, at the north end of Lake Nyasa, and there were now three stations in the hills among the Abangoni, at Njuyu, at Hora and at Ekwendeni. News floated up also of the increasing number and

Citizenship

power of the Europeans in the Shire Highlands, and that there a representative of the Queen had been stationed with some Indian soldiers, who were already fighting with the Arabs and other war-makers. These things all acted as a brake on the old fury of the warriors and successfully blocked the ways where formerly they had driven headlong.

To-day we can see how numerous were the influences which were changing the habits of the people, but to the Abangoni the one recognisable cause was the mission in their midst, with its disciples who preached against war, and its multiplying schools which daily taught the things that make for peace.

Daniel Mtusu was one of the most ardent and useful of the new disciples. His social status as well as his energy singled him out from the others. In spite of those who called him a rebel he remained a most loyal citizen, only discarding and denouncing with the rigour of a recent convert customs which he recognised to be opposed to Christian teaching. He had not broken with beer drinking, though he personally ceased to drink to excess. He still hoed his fields with the help of beer feasts, but he and the other young Christians soon came to realise that beer drinking was the cause of a great part of the violence in the tribe. In his own field or village the feasts began with great jollity, but by night pandemonium was let loose, resulting in quarrels, infidelities and the bitter fruits of inflamed passions.

It was not long until he and his fellow-Christians saw that they could only fulfil their duty to the State and guard themselves from temporary lapses by abstaining altogether from beer. So they set for themselves a self-denying ordinance and agreed that the rule of the Church should be that of total abstinence from intoxicating drinks. They still retained the custom of community hoeing, but now they prepared maize porridge, killed one or two goats and called the neighbours together. This sober service was given with no decrease of jollity, and, when the evening came, self-respecting people returned to the village quietly, leaving behind them a vastly better cultivated garden than they would have done had they been hoeing for beer.

The great athletic and social amusements of hunting and the *ingoma* dance were maintained as vigorously in Daniel's village as anywhere else. On moonlight nights Daniel danced in the kraal and sang his loudest. When the cold season came he and his young men and maidens went forth gaily dressed to dance all day in competition with other villagers. But he saw to it that no immoral songs spoiled the joy of the day and that his party returned home while the sun was still shining.

He had now entered into his full manhood, and had to take his position as village head. Hours were spent in his own village listening to interminable cases, and when he was called into the common council of the Hoho group he took his place and helped to give judgment without fear or favour.

One day there came a request for protection from a Lake-shore chief, named Ngombo, whose people had often been raided by Hoho and who had secured peace years before by becoming tributary to Hoho. Ngombo had come to recognise the measure of security that was now creeping over the land, and, finding that—while the Lake still supplied abundance of fish, the narrow strip of land on which they cultivated cassava was worn out and was ceasing to produce sufficient food, he resolved to push out some villages towards the foot-hills where the trees still grew on almost virgin soil. Yet it was a risky experiment to leave the stockaded villages of the shore and build in the " no man's land " which lay between the Lake and the country of the Abangoni. Restless parties who did not recognise the truce were apt to swoop down on helpless people and take their food and possessions, and kill those who resisted.

So Ngombo invited Hoho to come and give him protection until his new villages were erected. To this Daniel and many of the young men of his section who recognised their proprietary right over Ngombo's villages willingly responded. Here at least was a good field for their unexercised military spirit. Fully armed in the old fashion, not now to kill and steal, but to be a terror to evil-doers and help the unprotected, they sallied forth and, on arriving at the new sites, formed a guard round them. So long as they were there no venturesome and rash marauders dared to attack, so the pioneers hewed down the trees, turned the soil and aired it, and built the little huts which were to form their villages. When all this labour was over, and the people had settled into their new quarters, Daniel and his friends returned to the hills with the satisfaction of having done a good service.

Shortly after this a young lad belonging to Daniel Mtusu's village went mad and found his way down to the Lake shore. Daniel at once decided to follow him and bring him back, that he might be under his own care. But it was pointed out to him that he could not make this journey without grave risk, for some irresponsible bands of Abangoni had recently raided near the Lake shore and had burned villages and carried off captives. This breaking of the truce had awakened a spirit of retaliation, and the Atonga were ready to do hurt to any of the Abangoni whom they found in their midst. The possible risk, however, did not deter Daniel, and as he learned that the mad boy was at Ngombo's village by the Lake he determined to go there and fetch him back.

Now Ngombo was no longer friendly. He was angry that peace had been broken by the Abangoni, and, while he had got all the service he wanted from Hoho, he felt himself strong enough to have his revenge on any unwary visitor from the Red Land.

Accompanied by one or two friends, Daniel crossed the hills and made his way down to the Lake shore, arriving there on the second or third day. At Chinyenta's village, which stood close by Ngombo's old stockade, he was received in a friendly spirit and hospitably entertained. Here he prepared to spend the night, while his companions went on to other villages, not far off. Meanwhile Ngombo heard that one of Chipatula's sons was staying in the neighbouring town, and he began to form plans to get him into his power. Two or three head-men and Chinyenta were called to discuss his plot, and in the secret of his hut Ngombo proposed that they should kill Mtusu. But Chinyenta would not hear that any harm should come to his guest and strenuously opposed all that Ngombo proposed ; although he had rebelled and fled from Mombera he retained most friendly relations with the family of his old chief Chipatula.

Early next morning he told Daniel secretly that he was surrounded by enemies, who had determined to murder him, but that he would make it his business to save him in the hour of danger. With his

Citizenship

approval Daniel summoned his travel-companions together from the villages in which they were scattered and then went forth with him to visit Ngombo and make inquiries about the mad fugitive.

After a somewhat surly greeting and a little talk, Ngombo took Daniel by the hand and led him to the stockade which ran round his old village. On some of the poles the heads of Abangoni who had been killed years before were bleaching.

"Do you see these heads?" cried Ngombo. "Before the sun goes down your head also will be fixed alongside of them."

He then began to rouse himself to a fury before laying violent hands on the young man. Suddenly Chinyenta seized his guest and rushed him with some violence into a neighbouring hut and closed the door, shouting all the time to his friends to gather round him and defend him.

Ngombo was in no mood to fight within his own village and, finding that his immediate designs were frustrated, he went away, intending to seize Daniel by stratagem or by force the following day. But that night Chinyenta, who with his men had kept close guard over his guest, stealthily conveyed him and his friends out of the village and escorted them through the maze of paths that ran out and in among the fields and entanglements of bush until at last they arrived at the foot-hills.

As soon as they began to climb out of the hot, steamy levels, and Daniel felt again the firm, stony ground beneath his feet, he knew he was fit for any enemy who might seek his life, so he ordered his good friends to return to their homes and leave them to continue their journey alone.

"Now I can defend myself," he claimed. "If I

117

am attacked, I shall not die until I have slain two or three of my enemies."

For Mtusu was never a " passive resister." The old fighting spirit that was in him never learned to take an injustice quietly, and he stood bravely on more than one occasion to defend his own honour and the rights of his fellows.

Rejoicing to have come so safely out of a grave danger, and acknowledging the Hand of God in his rescue, Daniel continued his journey, climbing and descending the tree-clad hills until he emerged on the high wind-swept grasslands and at last arrived among his own people.

Chapter XIV

ADVENTURES

THE days of isolation when the warrior tribe sat secure surrounded by a wide buffer desert across which few but armed warrior bands might travel at last passed away. No convention of the tribes had been called to discuss treaties of peace and no " scraps of paper " had been signed by the contending parties. Yet peace had come : early in the 'nineties the last raid took place. Harvest time arrived ; the grain was carried to the barns ; but no war-party appeared to lift the fruit of the cultivator's labour. The stockade gates were still barred each night, but no village was startled in the early dawn by the yells of an attacking *impi*. Tacitly the people accepted the changed conditions, hardly aware when the peace had begun, and quite without guarantees from any authority that the old terror would not again arise.

Travellers now ventured to move along the narrow, winding tracks without fear of sudden attacks by hidden robbers. The children of serfs, who had been brought up among the Abangoni and had transferred their loyalty to their new surroundings and people, now began to seek out their relatives among the

Adventures

neighbouring tribes and gradually to create friendly relationships between the raiders and raided. The fugitives and harried people came out of their fastnesses and built unprotected villages on richer and healthier ground, and in an almost incredibly short time the wild days became the history of a nightmare. By '95 the Atonga and Achewa and Basenga and other broken people spoke loudly of their valiant deeds on the field, remembering only their victories and forgetting all their defeats and sufferings, while the Abangoni saw their head-dresses rotting on the tree-tops and told stories of their invincible might, forgetting their treacheries and surprise tactics and bloody cruelty, but remembering the glory of this regiment and that. Neither the raiders nor the raided retained bitterness or hatred. Intermarriage in the land of the conquerors between the children of the masters and the children of the slaves was rapidly moulding the tribes into friendly and related peoples.

Now that no wealth came by marauding it was necessary that men should work. Parties of Abangoni wandered down to the Lake shore to find employment with the agents of the trading companies, who sent them to Blantyre by the sore and humiliating passage of the Lake to carry loads and to labour in the coffee plantations. There they soon found themselves under Atonga foremen, for the Atonga had been among the first to respond to the new civilisation, and their natural brightness made them acceptable and useful to the Europeans. But these recently emancipated people were the most exacting of foremen, and it was no easy, though necessary, obedience that their Abangoni labourers rendered them. They dared not retaliate, for the foremen were backed by

NATIVE GIRLS WINNOWING

A GIRL COOKING MAIZE PORRIDGE

The earthenware pot is held steady by her feet. A basket of
meal is by her side.

Adventures

the prestige of the white masters; and even should they on their return plan revenge, all power of combination had been lost and no war-party could be summoned. Besides, they had seen enough with their own eyes to know that the white rulers would not passively suffer a recrudescence of the raiding days.

When the paths were opened and made safe for those who wished to use them, Daniel became a great traveller. He had relatives and friends up and down the Red Land; he even had relatives who had settled near the Lake itself among the former allies and tributaries of the Hoho people. For eight months in the year he was more or less tied to his work as a teacher, though the week-ends were free for movement and for hunting. It was during the holiday months that he found time and opportunity for crossing the borders of his own land and finding his way to the shores of the Lake.

At such a time he was walking along with a party of others on the path that led to the Atonga country. He had already crossed the hills and descended to the plain, but night fell before he had arrived at his destination, so he and his friends were pressing on quickly for the nearest village. Suddenly they saw two lions standing on the moonlit path some distance ahead. But this did not cause them to slacken their pace. With defiant shouts they continued their rapid march, drawing nearer and nearer to the lions. Of course, Daniel and each of his friends were armed with their shield and spear, which they carried now to protect themselves against wild beasts. The lions, seeing the fearless advance of the travellers, took flight, bounded along the path and were quickly lost to sight.

Adventures

Coming in the opposite direction were two other belated wayfarers, a man and his wife, who in turn found themselves suddenly confronted with the bounding lions. At the sight of this awful apparition the husband forgot all his sense of chivalry, fled for his life, and left his laden wife terror-stricken on the path. In her fear she shrieked loudly again and again.

Through the silence of the night, to Daniel and his party, who were laughing over the success of their bold fronting of the lions, there came the sound of the woman's terror. They knew at once what had happened, and raising the old war-yell rushed to the rescue. When the lions heard and saw these bold and shouting attackers they found their safety in instant flight.

The woman's gratitude to her deliverers was immense. When she told her story, Daniel went to seek for her runaway husband, whom he soon found ingloriously hiding in the branches of a tree. He was brought down, while the whole party jeered mercilessly at his base desertion of his helpless wife.

Hunting is one of the best and healthiest sports of the Abangoni. After the grass is burnt, big drives are organised, and on Saturdays especially Daniel used to join these hunting parties. Dressed only in two skins hung about his loins, carrying a small shield and a spear and knobkerrie, from early morning to evening he would lead the chase. Numerous lean dogs accompanied the men and were useful in running down the quarry. Sometimes two or three small buck were killed; occasionally one of the larger antelopes. The real excitement, however, was when they came on the track of a leopard or a lion. Then pluck and stout courage were necessary for

Adventures

men who were only armed with weapons that killed at close quarters. Encounters with fierce beasts of prey might only be the accident of a safe run after buck, but they were also the deliberately planned adventure of men who sought to destroy the beasts that were harassing their flocks and herds.

In the early days of the mission Daniel once borrowed a shot-gun from the Kaffir teacher who was stationed at his village and went to shoot duck in the pools of the Kasitu. As he crept along through the reeds he suddenly found himself face to face with a great python. Thinking he could easily kill it with his shot-gun, he fired, but only wounded and irritated it. The great snake leapt at him, seeking to envelop him in its monstrous folds, and Daniel tripped and fell on his face before it. But in its leap the snake seems to have been obstructed by a shrub. This gave Daniel time to shout for help and get out of the danger zone. One or two lads who had been following close behind him dashed to his help, and the python turned and disappeared among the reeds.

Some time after this Daniel had a serious illness, and lay at home recovering very slowly. Night after night the village had been disturbed by a leopard which had taken one or two dogs, and had broken into the goat pen and killed several goats. To rid themselves of this dangerous raider the people arranged for a careful hunt. In the morning Daniel had been sitting about very languid and weak from his recent illness, but the sight of the gathering men and dogs and the prevailing excitement of the chase were too much for him, so he announced that he must join the others. His friends protested that he was unfit for so arduous a day, but he declared that the movement and fun of the hunt were the best medicine for a convalescent.

Throwing aside his blanket, he donned his skins and set forth with his shield and spear. The hunters had not gone very far when the dogs roused a leopard. As soon as he saw it, Daniel shouted, "This is my prize! He has killed my goats and dogs." Sickness and weakness were forgotten. The only thing that mattered now was the flashing, dangerous robber of the kraals, there before him, but moving off into cover, stealthily, rapidly.

Off dashed the invalid, yelling, whistling, shield and spear high in the air, mad with the lust of the chase. Foti, a younger brother, and the hunting dogs followed close after, and then the whole party. Foti soon passed Daniel and was the first to come up with the leopard. When Daniel arrived, panting and wild with excitement, he found Foti and the dogs holding the leopard at bay. Just at that moment it gathered itself to spring, but Daniel seized his brother and threw him behind his back. This stopped the beast's intention.

Then Daniel began to defy it and to challenge it after the fashion of hunters. "Don't attack small boys!" he cried. "Here am I, a full-grown man. Come at me." With the taunt he rattled his club on his shield and glared defiance.

The leopard accepted the challenge at once and sprang on Daniel, lacerating his hand and foot. Swift as lightning Daniel struck with his knobkerrie and hit the leopard a tremendous blow on the head, knocking it down and stunning it for a moment. But he lost his balance in the fury of the blow and fell to the ground also. Immediately the beast turned over and caught his right hand, tearing it badly.

Adventures

Foti, however, was there, trying to get his share in the fight, and when the leopard seized Daniel, he leapt forward and drove his spear into its side. At the same time another man arrived, smashed the brute's head with his axe and killed it.

The hunters were soon dancing about their fallen prey, and after lashing it to a branch which they cut from a tree, they carried it home in triumph, Daniel following behind.

With song and dance they marched round the kraal of the head village, filed through the narrow gateway and laid the carcase down on the dry manure. Then Daniel, forgetful of his weakness and the pain he was suffering from his wounds, danced in pantomime the whole story of the fight. That day his hand and foot swelled up dreadfully. The wounds were badly poisoned. Day by day his sores were dressed by the mission doctor, and this painful operation he bore without a murmur. At last he was healed, but his hand and fingers remained twisted and cramped all the rest of his life. That perhaps gave him a good excuse for atrociously bad writing, which was always a characteristic of his.

Chapter XV

THE TEACHER

IS HERE IN HIS BEGINNINGS, AND SIMPLICITY, TOGETHER
WITH A SKETCH OF HIM OPENING A NEW SCHOOL

FROM the day of his conversion to the day of his death Daniel was a mission teacher. He was also a head-man, controlling the affairs of his own village ; a cultivator, growing all the year's food for his household ; a householder, building his own house and barns and keeping them in repair. But to native and European alike his profession was that of a " mission teacher."

At first his knowledge and training were so elementary that no one could claim he increased the prestige of education in the land. But the hopeful element in his character was that, although he was now a married man, the road of progress was not closed against him, and year by year he grew in knowledge and power. It was well that a fair seniority was on his side, for his scholars were not all children. The young men and young married women who frequented it and who brought with them, by more than moral suasion, the children of the village, were the backbone of the school. It was necessary that the teacher should be a man of some social standing and of experience.

Not that Daniel, or any other teacher, was ever allowed to use physical punishment to maintain

The Teacher

discipline. Life was too complicated for that. For if a teacher struck a child for a fault, not only would the culprit escape by the open door, but a goodly part of the class would go with him ; and then the mothers, uncles and fathers of the aggrieved one would have endless causes for the village court against the teacher. Parents might still retain and exercise their powers of discipline, especially if the herd-boys allowed the cattle to wander into other people's gardens, but no outsider could touch another's child. Besides, should any accident or sickness befall the punished one, though it were months afterwards, the resentful relative would quickly trace the trouble back to the punishment by the irate teacher, and then " the fat would be in the fire."

Moral authority therefore was the only power which could maintain the discipline of a school, and of this Daniel had his share. He began his profession as a monitor, that meant he had the task of teaching the alphabet class. For this he was supposed to have enough knowledge, because he could read the Scriptures in his own tongue in a halting fashion. He had no idea of method, and his only system was a long pointer and constant repetition by the class in unison. When forty or fifty grown-ups and youngsters roared simultaneously the letters of the alphabet there was a joyful sound in school and in the neighbourhood. The marvel is that after a time a percentage mastered the mystic signs. A weary, monotonous job this for an intelligent man, you may think. But the African has unlimited power of reiteration, and just because he does not stop to analyse what he is doing he feels that he is working.

When I arrived in the Red Land at the beginning

The Teacher

of 1897 to reap what others had sown, Daniel had attained to something like the second or third standard, and was now a teacher in charge of a school. The mission was moving out of its pioneer stages. Dr. Laws had just opened an institution on a high, uninhabited plateau overlooking the Lake, where he hoped to carry selected youths through a thorough training in pedagogy and prepare the leaders of the new nations that were to be.

Many a time the Abangoni armies had skirted this plateau in the olden days until they had swept it and its neighbourhood clear of villages. Beneath a waterfall, in caves from which a sheer precipice fell away, the doctor found some terrified folk who still clung to the land of their fathers. High up on the steep mountain-side, six and seven thousand feet above sea-level, little clusters of huts were built, from which the inhabitants could run like rabbits when they saw the enemy approach.

Right in the heart of this desolation the institution was founded, and it has since grown into a huge training centre, surrounded by prosperous and progressive villages.

Among the first to apply with great eagerness to be taken on as a pupil was Daniel, the alert and ambitious young Christian. But he was not allowed to go there, for the opportunity of extending schools in the Red Land was now too inviting, and there were not enough reliable men to carry them on.

So to his bitter disappointment Daniel was sent back to conduct a village school, terribly conscious of his own unfitness and of the great fields of knowledge that lay before him untilled.

Towards the close of 1897 Mr. Stuart and I made a tour among some of the important chiefs, trying,

The Teacher

with a measure of success, to get their permission to open schools for their people. The most interesting opportunity that was given us came through the invitation of the young paramount chief, who had only been appointed a few months before, after the mission had brought strong pressure to bear on the *indunas* (councillors). He, from some sense of his own inexperience and of the complications which were arising through the presence of white men in the land, willingly accepted our offer of a teacher, and we placed Daniel with him, along with his devoted friend, Andrew.

As soon as it was known that the great chief had a school, a most urgent request that would accept no denial came from his brother Chinde, who had moved into new lands in the west. Next year, in February, taking two teachers with me, I travelled out to see this fresh opening, and, passing through the great chief's village, carried off Daniel to introduce me to Chinde and help me in my interview. After journeying further west for five or six hours we arrived at Chinde's head village. We had a great reception, and as Daniel had been an old friend of this chief, he was doubly welcome.

Seated on logs in the great cattle kraal we successfully carried through our first interview, I in wooden fashion trying to make my remarks, while Daniel in his own fluent and winsome way interpreted, through words that could be understood, all that I tried to say.

Handsome gifts of cattle, goats and fowls were given to me as a welcome, and through the intricate courtesies to be observed in accepting the gifts Daniel guided me step by step.

That night I witnessed for the first time one of

the great dances of the people of the soil. It was not an *ingoma*, healthful and clean, which the Abangoni loved, but one of those debased dances which turned the moonlight nights into foul obscenity.

When I arrived on the scene the dance had been some time in progress and was decent enough ; but when the people warmed to the fun of it, it grew more and more vile. Daniel was there standing by me. But what he saw did not affect him as it did me. Now and then he interposed to say that some things were not proper, but I had recently come out of the atmosphere of Christian Scotland, and he had lived in the atmosphere of pagan Africa, so the shock which was mine was not his.

Next morning I spoke to the assembled people of the horror of the night. All I said was emphasised by Daniel. He, too, knew that these things should not be done, and, strange to say, the old Abangoni also agreed that the dances of the slaves were unfit and were destroying the village morality. So I asked that, if a school were placed here, there should never again be a repetition of the scenes of the previous night.

That same day Daniel began the work in Chinde's village. There was no need to wait for a building or for any school appliances beyond the alphabet sheets with which we had come provided, for the whole community was at one stage—the stage of knowing nothing.

In the midst of a clearing in the wood the school was opened. The fallen logs were drawn aside and placed in some relation to one another so as to provide seats for the pupils and give some appearance of order to the gathering. Above were the branches of trees which provided shade and formed the

The Teacher

majestic roof of the school. Beneath was the sand, clean and slightly covered with short grass. Beyond was the village, not too near to disturb the exercises of the school, and not too far to forbid the most indolent to approach and at least look on, or hear what the teacher might say.

Here before two or three hundred pupils of all ages, wearing a common uniform of dark skin only, varied in the case of the elders by the addition of little pelts of antelopes and monkeys, and in the case of the children by a few seed beads, Daniel Mtusu stood as the teacher and leader of those who would follow him into the paths of knowledge and life everlasting.

If you would estimate his value as the pioneer of education in this dark forest land, compare him with those whom he would teach. He has assets that the most highly trained teacher from Europe cannot have. For he stands there one of the people themselves. Everybody knows him and his father's house, his proved valour in war, and his great renunciation. He speaks their own tongue, has their outlook and background too, thinks their thoughts and expresses them in the forms that they appreciate. And yet, what a difference even on the surface of things ! They sit around, a naked and unwashed throng. He stands among them dressed in clean calico, and his body has the bright, healthy look of one who is not unacquainted with soap and water. He holds in his hands a Bible and hymn-book, the printed page, which to them utters nothing but to him speaks with a living tongue. They sit terrified when they see the formidable and unaccountable forces of nature—life, death, disease, lightning, earthquakes—unable to understand what all these things mean. He lives in

The Teacher

a calm faith that God is his Father and lovingly holds in His Hand the world and all who dwell therein.

There is contact there between him and them, yet he reaches out far beyond and in front of them. Let him declare the things he knows, and he will give a treasure infinitely above the price of his wages of three shillings a month, a treasure well worth the pains endured, and the lives laid down by European missionaries that such as he might be.

The school opens with a hymn. No one knows the words or the music, for we had not yet reached the time when we drew the haunting native tunes into the service of God. So Daniel chose the simplest of all hymns, and the one he sang on the day of his great vision. It is so simple they can all remember the first verse, " Come to Jesus just now, Just now come to Jesus." Again and again he repeats it until all remember it. Then he sings it once, and asks them to join at the second line. What a noise and discord arise ! No one has caught the strange rhythm of this English music. Again and again they sing the first verse until a slight resemblance to Daniel's version is discovered. Then he gives them the second verse and repeats it again and again. So they move slowly and painfully through the opening hymn. Its words are mystery and must remain so for a long time. Who Jesus is they know not, not even that this is the name of a Person. Some perhaps think it is another name for a school. Nor do they understand what is meant by " coming to Him." But here is the first of the foreign magic which they must learn. By and by they will understand. When the singing is over there is an immense amount of chattering and laughing, and attempts to hum again the first verse, till Daniel calls for silence, and explains

The Teacher

that he is now going to pray, so all must bow their heads and close their eyes.

Why close their eyes? Some try it for a moment and then open them. Others hide their eyes with their hands and laugh aloud as they peep through between their fingers and see the twisting of features of those who try to keep their eyes tight. But others look behind them to see that no one at the back will do them hurt if they shut their eyes. At last there is silence and Daniel begins to pray. Here he is far in front of them all now, for he knows how to speak to God. But he has only said a few words when discussion and restlessness break out again, and some of the more knowing ones call loudly for silence. The noise does not disturb the simple prayer of the teacher and he goes on until he has completed what he has to say.

Now the school is ready for its first lesson, and that must be the Bible lesson. This day Daniel does not attempt to take a story from the Bible. The first words are his first text, " In the beginning God." And he tells them something about God that they never knew before. He is too much inclined to preach. He has not yet learned how to lead them on step by step from the things they know to the next things they should know. But he has uttered the great word and told them that God is the Creator of the world and is in it to-day.

When this lesson is over the whole school is turned into an alphabet class. Pointing to the first letter, Daniel explains that is it called " ā." Then he asks them to say " ā." With a shout the three hundred respond and roar " ā." They must repeat it, and joyfully and with full lung power they do so. They have learned a ridiculous new song, and " ā " is repeated again and again. Few look at the sheet. The sound has no relation to the printed symbol—it is just a song. The old people sitting and kneeling on the outskirts laugh, and smile approvingly at the wisdom of the pupils. This new magic of the European is very jolly, and when " b " comes it is just as funny. Is this " Chinglezi "—the language of the Europeans?

It is all very amusing, and very bright, and perfectly harmless. Why should anyone object to a school? Let the children learn these new songs!

On goes Daniel, diligently plodding to the very end of the sheet until the class has ceased to look at his pointer, and are roaring the new chorus he has taught them. It has been a morning of confused sounds and much energy, and when the lesson is over everyone feels that he has worked hard. But no one is any the wiser.

However, the school has begun. On succeeding days the teachers whom we shall leave behind us to conduct the school will not be so ambitious to cover the whole ground. Each day they will insinuate some new knowledge of God, some new ethical command, and light will steal into the minds of those who really want to know. The house, too, must be built in which they will learn, and, as soon as possible, all the scholars will set to work cutting trees, clearing the ground, hoeing and tramping clay, until one day a decent and tidy house to learn in will stand as the pride of the village.

That evening I sat with the teachers in a hut and spoke of the things that were to be. Next morning early I left them alone there to prepare a sweet and fruitful garden of the Lord.

Chapter XVI

PIONEERING

IN THE SAD, BUT FASCINATING, LOANGWA VALLEY, WITH
DANIEL AS GUIDE AND PREACHER, OPENS
NEW FIELDS OF SERVICE

CONSTANT extension was now the mood of
the mission. Head-men and chiefs accepted
the fact that the days of war were over, never
to return, and they began to adjust themselves to the
new conditions. The young men recognised that
education greatly increased their value and wages in
the labour market and their prestige in the community. The chiefs became nervous about their
increasing contact with Europeans and wished to
have by them a teacher who had some knowledge of
the European and his ways and could read letters
that might come to them. What with the necessities
of state and the economic stimulus, to say nothing of
the mere undefined desire to know the truths of the
evangel, requests began to pour in from all sides that
we should open schools and send teachers.

Of course, our power of producing reliable men to
carry on a school of even the simplest sort was limited.
Neither the needful intelligence nor character was
produced mechanically to enable us to send men as
each fresh opening occurred. To sift the applications
we were able to add new conditions of self-help for
those whose invitation might be successful. Thus we

Pioneering

began to require that a school-house, fees from the scholars and food from the people for the stranger teachers, should be promised, before we could answer any call.

As for the production of teachers, an increasing number of young men who had made profession of Christianity were eager for this, the only vocation for them in the land. The more promising of them were chosen to be monitors and were given instruction daily at the various stations till they made some advance. The teachers, too, were frequently called in to the stations and taught there. By constant visitation of the out-schools, and by means of these schools for teachers, our scattered helpers were kept fairly faithful and progressive.

At each visit I paid to his school I found Daniel in great form, with visible fruits of his work. A good pole-and-mud house was standing : the pupils attended in large numbers : the young chief himself was making some progress, though sadly handicapped by his royal vices. Village manners were mending somewhat and evil dances had been suppressed. A few lads and girls had joined the Enquirers' Class, and Daniel was giving them special instruction.

Wandering among those villages in the west one began to ask what lay still further west, beyond the great stretch of woods and hills, down in the valley of the Loangwa, and one was told of a people called the Basenga who lived in big, stockaded villages, and at one time provided a happy hunting-ground for some sections of the Abangoni.

When I mentioned to Daniel my desire to visit those people, he expressed his eagerness to accompany me. He had already been through the southern part of the valley with the army, and he knew a good deal

Pioneering

about the various chiefs of the Basenga. There were no paths by which we might travel, for long years of war had closed all communication between the Abangoni and the Basenga. But we were fortunate in finding two native elephant hunters who offered to guide us over the wilderness.

Leaving Andrew in charge of his school, I took Daniel with me, and for the next two or three days we travelled through woods, and down stony waterless hills, until we came to the great valley.

Our visit caused some alarm at first, for my carriers were all Abangoni, and these people had never been in the valley before except for plunder. But Daniel had one great word for all, that the " Word of God " had conquered the Abangoni and they had come to speak it to the Basenga.

The language of the people is very similar to that of the Batumbuka who comprised the greater number of the serfs of the Abangoni, so Daniel was able to speak with them at once, and before much time had elapsed he could be seen sitting at ease with some of the men carrying on a conversation which might last for hours. They talked about the old days, and gave news of men whose names were known to them. They talked about the growing and weaving of cotton, an art then known to the Basenga, but now forgotten, and Daniel would sit for long periods watching the weavers at work. He was not slow to appreciate the arts in which they excelled and of which the Abangoni knew nothing, and to let the people see his admiration of their skill.

When the villagers gathered to hear our worship, everyone was present, but at a distance. None yet ventured too near the white man and his carriers. I always spoke a little in Chingoni, though I knew that

Pioneering

only a very few could understand the simplest things in this most foreign language. Then Daniel rose to restate what I had said and to pour forth a full-dress sermon.

I see still my herald preaching in an old, filthy village, while I sat beside him on a chair at the tent door. Around us were the dusty, rat-infested huts. The ground beneath our feet was sandy, loosened by the constant tread of human feet, and round among the huts gusts of wind came blowing, blinding us and covering with dust our persons and belongings. A fierce sun shone overhead through the great thorn trees that surrounded the stockade and stood here and there about the village. The people sat in the shade of the huts, choosing their place not for convenience of hearing or to form a compact audience, but for coolness and sight. Here twenty women and girls sat on the sand ; there thirty men ; away in the distance twenty or thirty children, and so on. They distributed themselves where shade gave ease and distance security.

Facing this broken crowd stood Daniel, clothed in a shirt and a piece of white calico. His head and his feet were bare ; his light brown skin contrasted with the dirty black of the unwashed Basenga. His eyes flashed with a great earnestness, but he had not yet acquired that ease and mellowness which came to him in later days and let him smile and look tenderly on the people.

His lithe, small body was never still as he paced here and there after the manner of the orators in the kraal. His hands moved in graceful, interpreting action. To the most distant his clear, tense voice could reach, and sometimes far beyond.

He had begun by telling the Basenga of the change

that had come over their old enemies. He saw no other cause but that which had beaten him down, "The Word of God," and he urged that they, the oppressed, should learn the word that had altered their oppressors. Then he began to pour out his Gospel. I fear it was a hard message he gave, denouncing their sins and ignorance and telling of certain judgment. "Destruction, destruction, destruction" were the words that were shouted again and again, but to a people who heard listlessly and without impression.

He spoke in Chitumbuka interspersed with a few Chisenga idioms which he had picked up since we arrived in the valley. But when he prayed he had to use Chingoni, for he knew not how to clothe his language to God in Chitumbuka.

For all of us the journey was peculiarly interesting and pathetic. The great, hot valley, waterless, covered with huge trees and alive with game, fascinated us more than anything we had seen in Africa. The miserable condition of the people, poverty-stricken, sickly, timid, still hiding in their filthy stockaded villages, dreading their enemies, touched our pity. One song with haunting minor music I heard them sing, "We are the trees of the Abangoni, made to be cut down." It was good to see that all through that journey Daniel was feeling that he and his nation had some responsibility for their misery. In village after village he urged that they be allowed to make some compensation by sending them teachers, and he did this so effectually that we were followed by urgent requests, that would take no denial, that the Abangoni themselves should come to teach and open schools.

Chapter XVII

BEULAH LAND

IS SHOWN TO DANIEL DURING A GREAT CONVENTION, AND
THE CALL TO MISSIONARY SERVICE IS HEARD

A FEW months after our visit to the Marambo, as the valley of the Loangwa is called, we held at Ekwendeni the first of our great annual Conventions, or sacramental gatherings. This was in the year 1898.

The people around the various schools were called to come together for five days' teaching and to bring with them thank-offerings to God. The idea was new, and great interest was created. We prepared long booths in which our visitors might sleep and cook their food. In the space between Mr. Stuart's house and the school we set up a brick platform with a grass shade overhead, and enclosed the two open sides of the space with a grass screen.

On the day before the opening of the Convention the people began to arrive, filing over the hill-sides laden with food for the coming days, and driving or carrying their thank-offerings with them.

Daniel was there with an immense company of his disciples. As he passed the outskirts of villages during the two days' journey, men sat on the ant-hills wondering what the stir was all about. They cried out, " Where is the army going ? " And Daniel shouted back, " It is the army of the Lord, going to hear the words of the King."

Some thousands of people were present throughout the Convention and, although but few of them were yet Christians, one message was spoken, reiterating the need of full surrender to God and ending with a word on the Holy Spirit.

The teachers were housed in a long, low brick building which was once a cattle-kraal, but was now used for boarder pupils. In the evenings Mr. Henderson, the head teacher of the Institution (now Dr. Henderson of Lovedale), who was helping us at this Convention, went with us to meet the teachers, and, sitting on the floor along with them, we talked over again the truths that had been uttered at the public gatherings. These little meetings were extraordinarily intimate and impressive. When we engaged in open prayer at the close, Daniel was always one of the first to take part. The prayers were not formal, but hesitating and deep with feeling. Once or twice towards the close they were broken with the sobs of those who prayed.

This was a new experience for us. Emotional expression of this sort was no common thing for the Abangoni, and it revealed to us that something more than intellectual assent was being given to the preaching.

Sunday was a notable day. The crowds were immense, for even the most ignorant heathen knew that this was the great day of the feast. In the forenoon we had the Lord's Supper, when a little company of Christians celebrated the sacred rite amid a sea of onlookers who sat silent and awed.

The afternoon was given over to a missionary session. Then we spoke not only of the untouched villages in the Red Land, but told the story of the journey to the Basenga. It seemed a rash thing to do. We were yet but a little company of Christians in the midst of a great population of heathen. Surely our first duty was to those near us, our own countrymen, and that required an effort sufficient to call up more than all our resources.

But the Abangoni had recognised no national limitations in their old fighting days. Half the continent had been their missionary field. Now as I asked for volunteers to bring peace to the Basenga they remembered a people whom they had raided and ruined. No sooner had I spoken than up rose Daniel's brother in the midst of the congregation and cried, " I have been out with the war-parties. I have plundered the Basenga and taken their cattle. Let me make some amends and go with the word of Peace and Salvation."

His ready offer drew one and another of the senior teachers to follow his example, and soon half a dozen of our most trusted men were on their feet offering their lives for the Basenga.

That day we launched our first missionary effort. The critics of our policy have long since been silenced. The daring enterprise put heart into those who worked among their own people, increased their zeal for extension, and at the same time claimed and won yet another tribe for the Kingdom of God.

Next morning we had our closing session, one of deep thankfulness, and then the people dispersed to their homes. If anyone doubts the value of such a gathering, he can see it in the history of the tribe, in the immense impact the whole dramatic demon-stration had on heathenism, in the deepening of Christian life and experience, and in the corporate

Beulah Land

sense that was given to the little scattered Church of
Christ. In the olden days the unity of the tribe used
to be expressed in the national gatherings for raiding.
Such meetings could no longer be held. Now the
unity of the tribe was to be expressed in the national
Christian Conventions, and that very act seemed in
some fashion to claim Christ as the dominant Power
among us.

No one had been more deeply moved than Daniel.
One had seen this in the evening prayers as well as in
his sheer joy in the public services. The people had
just dispersed, and I was sitting in my room, when I
was surprised by a visit from Daniel and his friend,
Andrew. They sat down on the mat, and without
preliminaries told me they had come to ask my advice
about experiences they had had, which they could not
explain. The two friends had been out together the
previous night praying in the bush. They had been a
long time in these exercises, enjoying great rapture of
soul, when they had seen angelic forms descending
and ascending. Their bodies, too, seemed to have
been lifted from the earth and floated about. (Such
experiences were not unknown to the mystics of
Europe.) Now the two lads wished to know what
these things meant.

I made no reply, but went through to the dispensary
which opened off my room, and took from a bottle of
salts two good doses, gave them each one and advised
them to have a sound sleep, and then we would talk
further.

If the visions faded, one is glad to believe that for
neither of these two men did the sense of their new
relation to God disappear. For that week's Convention and all that was said and done there had
tremendous value to them, and set them on a road

which was to lead to the ordained ministry and to make them notable interpreters of God's thoughts to men.

How good the months and years were which followed ! How sweetly the machinery of the mission now began to run ! What zeal and joy appeared in many a formal and listless one ! Drudgery was transformed into pleasant service, slacking into faithfulness. Distressing tangles became unravelled. The disturbing failures of human nature which so impede easy progress seemed to have gone, for jealousy, selfishness, gritty bickerings were all forgotten in the new colleagueship with God in which many had found themselves.

Of course, it must not be supposed that either Daniel or the other Christians remained on the heights to which they ascended without many descents and long dwellings on the cloud-covered plains. But they had stood where they had a vista of the glories of the Beulah land in which they might walk, and the memory of that can never let them be the men they were before they looked.

Months afterwards Daniel said to me, " The difference to us teachers is that we used to work when we feared the European's visit and his criticism of what we had done. Now we work knowing that God our Master is always seeing us and works along with us."

If he and the others could only retain in lively fashion this sense, what schools we might have in this mission ! But, alas ! the permanent attitudes are not always equal to the great moments. It would be a mistake if one gave the impression that Daniel was now a man who lived in the unvarying joy of his fellowship with God. He had a strong, emotional nature which made him capable of response to great movements ;

Beulah Land

but, if he had his times of elation, he had also times of depression, though, happily, not frequent or too prolonged.

For he was always a man of passion. Now it expressed itself in devotion to Christ and His Kingdom, but I have seen it express itself in wild anger and depressing sullenness. I have seen the dangerous light in his eyes when he was wronged, and the heavy, dull cloud of sulks, especially when anything touching his wages was not congenial.

The delightful thing about Daniel was that he was not an unfledged angel, but just a most ardent, lovable human, with many common weaknesses still clinging about him.

Chapter XVIII

A FILIBUSTER

ASSAULTS DANIEL, WHO DOES NOT SHINE AS A MEEK
CHRISTIAN

SO far no Europeans had settled in the Red
Land except the missionaries, and of these,
owing to various causes, there were now only
two unmarried men, both of whom lived at Ekwendeni.
The other two stations at Njuyu and Hora were under
the charge of native teachers. Then the time came
when I was the only resident European, for Mr.
Stuart had gone temporarily to the Institution.
Although a British Protectorate had been established
in Central Africa, the Red Land was left under the
control of its native chiefs, and the nearest British
resident was at Nkata Bay, among the Atonga.

Yet a passing European was becoming a fairly
common sight to the Abangoni, and wherever he
pitched his tent he was received with peculiar courtesy
and hospitality, especially if he showed in any way
that he was friendly with the mission. For the people
had come to recognise the missionaries as the repre-
sentatives of Europe, and attributed to them the
present peace and security.

Yet we consistently refused to hear civil cases, or in
any way to deal with matters which were within the
province of the chiefs. All we attempted was to
advise, especially when the interests of the people

146

A Filibuster

clashed with those of the Europeans. Government also used us as means of communicating with the chiefs should any difficulty arise.

But there was little to attract white travellers to the Red Land. Each year one or two came to recruit labour for the markets of the Shire Highlands, and they always paid their courtesy call at the mission first. By and by some young men wandered up from Southern Rhodesia and found their way to us to ask advice. We put them in the way of buying cattle, which they got in large numbers and at a very cheap price.

Rumours of their success induced others to follow in their footsteps, but they had learned from the pioneers a little of what ought to be done, and so did not find it necessary to come to the mission station for help. Our teachers were able to act as their interpreters and guides and showed to them the same friendly spirit which they had seen the missionaries show to the others.

One heard from native sources of these cattle-buyers and of one or two gold prospectors, and twice or thrice we had been called by native chiefs to assist in difficulties that arose with these latter.

The cattle-buying was good for the land, for there was an enormous number of beasts in the kraals and their sale brought calico in considerable quantities to the villages. But soon the market in cattle began to stiffen. People had sold enough and were demanding higher prices, till at last Europeans ceased to come.

By and by rumours reached me of a white man who was seizing cattle by force and raising a spirit of restlessness and resentment. Daniel, who was at home on holiday, sent me one or two letters telling me of this high-handed proceeding. At first I could not believe

A Filibuster

it, and thought that the story was possibly exaggerated by rumour. But as day by day it was confirmed by further tales, I wrote a note to Daniel, as a reliable teacher, to go and see with his own eyes what was happening and to report to me. On getting my letter he called two or three of his friends together, among others Andrew his inseparable friend, and David the impulsive.

They went first to Baleni's village, expecting to find the European there, but heard that he was camping near Julizga's, and thither they turned their steps. When they arrived at this village, they met Julizga's younger brother, whose body was scarred with the marks of the *chikote* (a whip of hippopotamus hide). They asked him how he had come by this severe thrashing, and he told them that Kanjechi (the name given by the people to the white man) had attacked him because he objected to being robbed of his cattle. So they invited him to accompany them to the stranger's encampment.

A little way beyond the village, on the hill-side, Kanjechi had set up his tent. Near it stood a large enclosure for the cattle, and all around were the booths of his carriers. A mob of cattle was being driven in for the evening, and Kanjechi himself stood at the entrance to their enclosure, counting them as they passed through. It took a long time, for an enormous number of beasts had been collected.

When they were all enclosed the white man, noticing the well-dressed group of lads waiting to speak to him, seated himself on a chair beside his tent and beckoned to them to come near and speak. The lads sat down on the ground near him, and immediately Daniel opened the talk, glad to find that Kanjechi could speak Zulu, which is very similar to Chingoni.

A Filibuster

" Are the people telling the truth," asked Daniel,
" when they say that you are taking cattle without
payment ? "

" Who told you that ? " cried the white man.

" I have heard it from many people, and here is
Julizga's brother all marked with the *chikote* because
he refused to sell to you."

This enraged Kanjechi somewhat, for here was a
" nigger " who was not afraid to speak frankly to him,
and who had been wise enough to bring evidences of
his charge.

" Who sent you to question me ? " he angrily asked.
" You must be mad."

Daniel replied that his master, Mr. Fraser, had
sent him.

" Well ! go and tell your master to come himself
to talk to me ! " shouted Kanjechi.

Thereupon Daniel instinctively rose, as if to go
with this message to me. But Kanjechi was now in a
passion, and when Daniel rose he took his *chikote* to
lash at him. Daniel did not cringe, but raised his
club over his head and caught the whip so that it did
not touch him. As the *chikote* came down on his club
with a smack, Daniel cried " Huwe ! " which might
be translated " Missed ! " It was the warrior's shout
when he turned aside a blow of the knobkerrie or a
thrust of the spear.

Again Kanjechi struck at him, but the defensive
club was up again, and again caught the lash, while
Daniel again shouted " Huwe ! " A third time he
struck, with the same result.

Now Daniel was no patient angel, and though
he stood upright and still before the attack of the
angry filibuster his temper was rising, and at the
third blow he shouted " Huwe ! " again, and let go

149

the rousing whistle of the warrior who is about to attack.

In a moment the other lads were on their feet, and two or three of them struck at the white man with their clubs, though Daniel took no action. Kanjechi raised his arms over his head and received the blows on them. Then passionate and impulsive David got in a great blow with his club on Kanjechi's head, and down the man dropped like a felled ox. Some would have beaten him as he lay, but Daniel stood over him and prevented them.

In a short time Kanjechi staggered to his feet, his face covered with blood, and whipped out his revolver. He could not see distinctly, but the white cloths of the lads were fairly visible, and he fired again and again, emptying his gun. David got a bullet in his hand, another lad had his leg pierced, and they scattered, running for their lives. Kanjechi then picked up his rifle and emptied its magazine on the fugitives, but without doing much harm.

Simon, a younger brother of Daniel, and two others fled for the river. When they reached it, they met some of Kanjechi's men returning with cattle. " Who is firing the shots ? " cried the men. " It is your master shooting birds," answered the lads with more slyness than truth. But the suspicions of the strangers were roused, and they exclaimed, " It is war. You have been trying to kill our master ! " and they lifted their guns to fire. A bullet grazed Simon's chest, and he fell to the ground. The men gathered about him to kill him, but he suddenly escaped out of their hands and fled through the thick bush.

Meanwhile Daniel and others had started off for Ekwendeni, where they arrived after a sharp trot of twenty miles with the blood of their wounds still unwashed.

After I had heard their story, I got food for them, and wrote a letter to the nearest magistrate telling him what had happened and asking him to come at once as there would certainly be mischief now. I sent on David and one or two other witnesses with this letter.

Meanwhile Kanjechi had become thoroughly alarmed. His head was badly hurt, and he knew enough of the people to be aware that as one had struck, others would follow his example. So that day he gathered his mob of cattle together, along with his carriers and belongings, and started in full flight for the south, he himself heading the rout.

Word soon passed that the white man and the cattle wrongfully seized were leaving the country. This was more than the independent Hoho people could allow, so next day an elder brother of Daniel called together a little party and started in pursuit of the cattle. They were not going to allow their possessions to leave the country without some attempt to regain them. After a rapid pursuit of some miles they came up with the rearguard of the fugitives, but Kanjechi himself was far ahead.

When the drovers saw the little armed party following, they fired wildly at any living thing. Unfortunately some villagers were near by, and three helpless women were killed by the firing. Then the drovers fled, and the carriers cast aside their boxes and, leaving the cattle to their fate, all made after their white master.

The Abangoni carefully gathered the cattle, and the boxes of gin and provisions which were scattered in the bush, and brought them in triumph to their

A Filibuster

village, where they were stored to be delivered over to the magistrate when he would inquire into the case. The rest of the story has already been told in my book, *Winning a Primitive People*. There you may read of the gathering *impis*, my difficult task in restraining them from pursuing and killing the white man, of the great meeting at the chief's kraal and the arrival of the magistrate, who took the matter in hand and, with a selected *impi*, followed hard, but unsuccessfully, after Kanjechi ; and, finally, of the trial by the British Commissioner of this infamous filibuster and of the light sentence which, with mistaken mercy, was passed on him.

But the months that elapsed before Kanjechi was tried at Ekwendeni were difficult ones for Daniel. All that he had done was natural and brave, but his friends, and David especially, had spoiled everything. Yet not a word of censure was passed on them by Daniel. He stood by them and rejoiced in their passionate loyalty. Indeed, no disclaimer would have any effect, for all the natives looked on him as leader and responsible for what had happened.

The timid, awed by fears of unknown consequences to the whole tribe, bitterly attacked Daniel. The white men would send guns and soldiers and wipe out the villages for the assault on one of their skin. Already the land of the great chief, Mpezeni (who ruled away south), brother of their own Mombera, had been seized by the Europeans, and all the cattle taken for some offence of which they were not surely informed. Soon the irresistible guns would be firing on their villages, and all the cattle in the kraals, their best treasure, would be taken from them.

Thus men talked in the kraals, and to Daniel's ears

A Filibuster

the conversation was reported. "Daniel," they said, "has ruined our country. He has roused war with the Europeans, and a white man has been hit on the head. If they come with an army, the land of the Abangoni will be taken, and many will be killed because of Daniel."

This was an ugly situation for him. He was quite conscious that David had done a most rash and evil thing, but he must bear the consequences, for he was responsible for what his friend had done. And he was not at all sure that disaster would not follow for his tribe.

Andrew found him in a state of great despondency, blaming himself for all the mess and dreading the worst evils. He who had so bravely stood alone in the dark days to do what was right, and had preached peace and called on the tribe to follow the new Way, was now the cause of all the trouble. Men did well to hate and denounce him.

The two friends spoke long together and Daniel revealed all that was in his heart and the black, dark thoughts he harboured. The end of it was that Andrew was able to persuade him that he must do himself no hurt, but trust that the Lord Jesus would overrule all the trouble in righteousness.

Then Daniel's soul recovered. Light and peace came back, and the talk ended by his declaring, "These are good words, and you have spoken the truth."

So when at last the trial was over and the filibuster punished, and the Abangoni commended for their restraint, there was no lighter heart in all the land than Daniel's, and he cried that "God had judged his case in righteousness by the mouth of His people and in harmony with His laws."

A Filibuster

For it was not punishment or revenge that he sought, but the declaration of what was right. And when the British Commissioner denounced this man as a criminal and an enemy of the Queen and all her intentions, he was sure that the judge was God's servant and spoke for Him.

Chapter XIX

AN ADVENTUROUS JOURNEY

TO THE SEA, WHICH BEGINS QUIETLY, AND ENDS WITH MANY RUDE SHOCKS

WHEN my time to go home on leave drew near several lads pressed me eagerly to take them with me to Scotland, and among these Daniel was one of the keenest. But it is an expensive item for a missionary to pay the passage and the hotel and other charges of a personal attendant. Neither is it a good thing to take one of these Central Africans, only recently lifted out of barbarism, and allow him to submit to the flattering attention of romantic people at home. Much as I should have liked to have my friend with me, it was neither wise nor possible to do so. However, as he had seen no lands beyond his own and the places to which he had accompanied the army, I decided to take him as far as the sea and let him receive what education there was in such travel.

It was a cheap and easy way to travel if he went as my personal servant, and, as this seemed no humiliation to him, but an honour to be sought after, he gladly accepted my offer and played his part well.

After we had crossed the familiar road to the Lake, and Daniel had spent full days with his friends and fellow-Christians at Bandawe, we embarked on the little steamer *Domira* and spent nearly a week in what was for Daniel a very novel and unpleasant method of travel. While we Europeans had the doubtful advantage of sleeping in cabins, stuffy and swarming with cockroaches, and of being served with regular meals, the crowded native passengers had only a very narrow deck space to themselves, and there they sat on fine days, were violently sick when the Lake was stormy, and slept in the quiet of the harbours where we anchored at night.

After leaving the turbulent Lake we sailed for two days down the Shire River and then disembarked near the Murchison cataracts and tramped across to Blantyre. Here I was the guest of the mission, and Daniel was received with great goodwill and made comfortable within the station. He saw now for the first time a really beautiful church set apart for the worship of God; wandered about in the township, confused with the coming and going of people who were all intent on their own business; discovered some of his fellow-tribesmen who were working on the plantations and who greatly rejoiced to see him; and spent hours with the leaders of the native church at Blantyre, discussing and disputing not a little over the small matters on which their usage differed from his.

We descended to the lower Shire after a few days, and again travelled in a flat-bottomed stern-wheeler down the Shire and the Zambezi. To me this was the most charming part of the journey, full of romantic interest, and more pleasant because I was now on my way home. I had my chair on a covered deck, my meals at a well-laden table, and my sleep in a bunk beneath a mosquito-curtain. But Daniel travelled like all other natives, sitting on the deck of the barge which was tied to the side of the steamer. The fierce sun blazed on his hatless head until it was westering and sent the shadow of the steamer over the barge. His meals could only be cooked when we tied up by the banks at night, and then he lay down on the ground beside a big fire along with the other native passengers and spent a dreamless night.

The whole voyage was full of great interest to him. There was the never-ending wonder of the river, and the villages, and the people standing by the banks. There was, too, the continual change in the manner of going, especially when we stuck on a sandbank. Then the noise and rage that came from the upper deck were terrible. For our skipper was too fond of whisky, and his orders, yelled with great ferocity, were very confusing. Frequently he shouted "Forward!" when he meant "Back!" for he was a little hazy about his vernacular words. When the flurried boat-boys pushed with their long bamboo-poles as he ordered, but not as he intended, a lump of firewood would come hurtling about their heads with mutterings about niggers not knowing their own language.

Under these tempests the poor native passengers cowered, but no harm was done them. For the skipper was really a decent, kind-hearted soul who could not keep calm in an emergency. One felt ashamed, however, and pained with the kind of introduction that Daniel was getting to one's fellow-countrymen.

Long before we had reached the Chinde mouth of the Zambezi I rather fancy that Daniel's longing to go on and see the lands of the Europeans had passed, for if some of the specimens he saw on the river were like the general type, life would be rather terrifying among them.

An Adventurous Journey

When at length we arrived at the Chinde township, which is a Portuguese possession, he was quite sure that there was no place like home and no government preferable to the British. For here he soon got into contact with Atonga lads who were serving the British Companies at Chinde, and the tales they gave him of the misrule of the Portuguese made the place seem like hell to a native. He saw the numerous wine shops into which lads were enticed and where they sat till they were fuddled with drink. He heard stories of the cruel punishments the Portuguese gave to natives guilty of slight or imaginary offences, and how quickly the wages earned slipped back into the officials' hands till the worker was impoverished instead of being enriched by his stay at Chinde.

Happily we did not remain long at this undesirable port, for the little ocean steamer that was to take me to Natal was lying there anchored in the river. When I went on board I was allowed to take Daniel with me and show him the wonders of the ship. He climbed the gangway, remarking that it was like going up Hora Mountain. We visited the engine-room and saw all over the ship, but it was my cabin that fascinated him. Here was a house within the great ship, and there were multitudes of others like it. He examined every item, and touched where he could. But in the whole wonder there was nothing that gripped him like the tip-up basins in the cabin. This little tangible convenience was more amazing than the engines, for he could grasp its meaning. He pressed the tap and the water flowed. He tipped up the basin and the water disappeared without messing the floor. All day long he would have stayed playing with this wonderful toy.

But the time had come when we must part. So I

An Adventurous Journey

saw him ashore, arranged for his passage back, and bespoke him some attention and consideration from the skipper of the river steamer on which he was to sail. It was not till years afterwards that I learned what a painful return journey he had, and then the story came not from himself but from his friend, Andrew.

On the way back to Blantyre he seems to have been kindly treated and thoroughly to have enjoyed the easy voyage. But he had only arrived at Blantyre when he was told that the steamer was to leave Fort Johnston in a day or two, and, if he wished to catch it, he must travel with all speed. As there might not be another steamer for a couple of months, it was necessary that he should catch this one and make haste to do so. The whole journey of about one hundred and twenty miles had to be made on foot and alone. The last stage was covered in the night before the steamer was to sail. It was dangerous for a lonely traveller to make the journey through the bush in the dark, but, as Daniel had no companion, and the steamer would not wait for him, he must perforce push on.

He had not gone very far that night when rain came on. It poured in torrents, and Daniel's thin calico was soon wet through and clung about him. The cold, merciless rain beat on him until his whole frame was shaking. There was no shelter in which he might take refuge and his only hope was to keep going.

He sang aloud the praises of God to keep his spirits up, and in the dark, long journey he felt he was not alone. But the cold was so great that he feared he could not live through it much longer, and he said to himself, " This is the last day of my life.

An Adventurous Journey

But what does it matter ? My soul is in the hands of God." The heavy rain at last ceased, and by and by his circulation was restored and he began to move along more comfortably.

Suddenly he heard two lions roar in front of him, for the Shire Valley used to be full of game, and lions were constantly abroad. The night was dark and moonless, so dark that he could not even see the road on which he walked. He prayed God that He would walk along with him that no harm might touch him, and so went rapidly on. As he drew near to the lions he stumbled against a hippopotamus that was feeding on the grass in the night. At first the hippopotamus did not see him, nor was it much startled by his touch, but, as soon as it got his scent, it gave forth a great bellow and plunged into the river. This was all the work of a minute. Daniel was alarmed when he stumbled against the creature, but, when it bellowed in his ear, he fell to the ground with fright. He was sure that it was a lion that roared, and that it was just about to seize him, and he cried to God to receive His servant.

But, when nothing happened, he recognised that the awful sound was not that of a lion, but of a hippopotamus, and he got to his feet, too shaken to be ashamed of himself or to see any humour in the situation.

He had not gone much farther when he knew that the lions were coming nearer and nearer to him. They kept up their fearsome roar that seems to terrify and silence all nature. At last he stood still, peering into the dark, and then the two forms loomed up before him. When they saw his white clothes they turned aside, and Daniel could hear the crackling of the grass beneath their feet as they slowly moved away

JUST MARRIED

The two bridegrooms are standing in the centre, second and third from the left, and before them are seated the two brides, second and third from the left.

An Adventurous Journey

from him. Then when he knew the road was clear he resumed his rapid walk.

At last the dawn began to break, and shortly after sunrise he arrived at Fort Johnston. There he found some Abangoni workers. But he stood before them shivering so violently with the cold wetting and all the excitement and fatigue of the night that he could not speak, and only stammered out his words.

The workers took him to their own sheds, where they kindled a great grass fire before which he warmed himself and recovered his speech. Meanwhile they had already placed a pot on their cooking fire and were getting some maize porridge ready. After he had eaten, all the misery of the night was forgotten as he chatted and laughed with his fellow-countrymen over his adventures.

That day Daniel got on board the little Lake steamer. But here all was bustle and confusion. Such a heap of boxes had to be stowed away and by such handless stevedores. Such a crowd of landward native passengers were blocking the decks that there was no getting about. The skipper was short-tempered, and the sun was hot, and the work to be done was most irritating.

Daniel unwittingly got in the way. The easiest method of clearing him out of the way was just to fling him aside. But in the passion of the moment the skipper miscalculated the power of his arm, and he shoved Daniel overboard so that he fell into the river. Happily the steamer was not far from the bank, for Daniel was not much of a swimmer; but he struck out for the shore, and just as he was about to touch it a crocodile rose up behind him and made for him. As he was but a stroke or two from the shore he escaped. But the horror of the crocodile was upon him, and he sat down on the bank, covered his face with his hands, and said to himself, "I shall never arrive back among my own people."

He was taken on board again. No apologies were made for his rough treatment, and the early part of the voyage was one long misery. The skipper was in a vile temper, and I fancy the very sense of the danger into which his passion had thrown Daniel, made him more irritable with him than with any of the other native passengers. Among the Europeans on board was the Rev. W. Murray, of the Dutch Reformed Church Mission at Mvera, a man whom I am proud to call a friend. When he heard that one of my teachers was on the ship, he sought him out, and found him. Now everything was changed, for here was a man who could speak with him and who showed a most loving and friendly heart. Through the remaining days Daniel travelled under the protection of Mr. Murray's friendship and found quiet and comfort.

Had Daniel told me of his adventures I should have been pained and ashamed. But I think he spared me the pain and the shame intentionally, for I never heard from him anything but interest in the new things he had seen and thankfulness for the experience.

To his native friends he often told the story of his return, not as a pathetic tragedy, but as a most comical adventure in which he did not shine as a hero, but as a poor, battered bit of helpless baggage.

Chapter XX

TEMPTING OFFERS

OF BETTER PAID WORK ARE MADE TO DANIEL, ONLY TO
BE REJECTED. THE MANNER OF THE LABOUR
TREK SOUTH IS EXPLAINED

ON his return home Daniel Mtusu immediately resumed his work as a teacher, content with very low wages and a very simple life. He felt that the wealth and elaboration of luxuries which he had seen in his travels had few compensations for the unfriendliness and exile in which they were enjoyed. The Red Land seemed more attractive, and his own people more delightful than any other land or people he had seen elsewhere, and the only white men among them, who were at the same time his employers, were kindly folk who knew and cared for him.

True his wages were almost contemptible. A few years ago he had been receiving six yards of calico a month—equal to about two shillings. Gradually he had risen to twelve yards. For calico was then the currency. There were no stores in all the Red Land where money could be exchanged for other goods, so a clumsy barter was the method of sale. A few seed beads represented a penny ; a live fowl, twopence ; a yard of calico, fourpence ; a sheep, three shillings, and so on. When workers received their pay, they had their choice of blue or grey calico, or a Madras cloth. When men would buy a school-book, they brought one or two live fowls, and for a Bible they brought a sheep. Payments and sales were elaborate business, and the recording of them in books a maddening vexation.

By and by we opened a little store, and began to pay in cash, for the worker now could exchange his money for what he wished. But it took a long time before cash was as popular as calico, and before men recognised that they were receiving real payment when they were paid with little silver or larger copper coins. As for gold, when a sovereign was offered for a cow, no one would take it, or, if some daring one did venture such a risky speculation, he expected to receive a note from the European certifying that he had come by the gold honestly.

Yet it must not be supposed that the few shillings which Daniel was paid were his whole wealth. That money only represented what he required to spend on luxury. He had no house rent to pay, for, like every other native, he built and owned his own hut. He bought no food, for in the rainy season, which was the long vacation time, he cultivated his own fields and produced all that was necessary for the year's meals. The mats to sleep on and the pots for cooking could be bought for a fowl from those who made them. There were no taxes to pay, for the country was not yet administered by the British Government. And withal he had cattle in the kraal, and goats in the pens, which were herded by the village youths without payment, and which had their annual increase, so that now and then he could afford to kill a beast for the entertainment of friends, or sell one, should he want to buy some luxury.

As the years passed and Daniel's intelligence and

training increased, his wages also grew in proportion, until he was earning what in this land is a good salary of about thirty shillings a month.

I do not think that money had a very high place in Daniel's thoughts, though I doubt if he was ever quite satisfied with the little wages he got. Once or twice in the course of his service there was some difficulty about his pay, when he thought himself entitled to an increase and the mission was unable to give it. Like all others he was peculiarly sensitive about anything that touched his salary. Work, and more work, might be given him ; he might be reprimanded, or allotted disagreeable duties, but these did not affect his spirits much. But, if you ventured to change his pay adversely, a dangerous mood was created. I have seen him in the most sullen and rebellious temper for days, because an unfortunate suspicion was uttered about his pay by the hurried and worried European who was dealing it out.

Yet he had plenty of tempting offers of better and higher wages. When European traders were travelling in the Red Land they often found the teachers of great help in advising and interpreting. A bright attractive man like Daniel, with a pleasant courtesy in his manner, who from the first had been in touch with Europeans, good and bad, naturally made many of these traders eager to acquire his permanent services. Happily, however, he was already wedded to his work of teaching from the highest motives, and he resisted all tempting offers.

One day such a man, who had benefited by his voluntary services, said to him, " What does the mission pay you ? "

" Five shillings a month."

" That's nothing," said the European, with great

contempt. "Come with me, and I will give you five pounds a month, and, if you prove helpful and trustworthy, your wage will be increased."

When Daniel showed no eagerness to jump at so liberal an offer, he was told to go away and think about it.

Next morning he returned to the trader and cheerfully cried, "I have thought about it."

The brightness of Daniel's tone made the trader sure that he was going to close with the tempting offer, and he replied eagerly, "Well! have you decided to come with me?"

"No!" said Daniel slowly. "Money is not everything. I must serve the Lord Jesus."

"Well! you are very foolish," was all the answer he got. I don't think the stranger meant for a moment to depreciate his motive, but he could not see anything but folly in choosing poverty rather than bright pecuniary prospects.

Unfortunately, all teachers were not so dedicated to their high service as Daniel was, and there was a continual drain on our most highly educated men, who threw up their work with us so as to gain the bigger wages that commerce and Government were ready to pay them. Had all these lads maintained a good Christian testimony, one would not have grudged their scattering far and wide. But I fear that, although the mission boys gained a fine reputation for cheerful diligence and efficiency, and for honesty and courtesy, too many of them fell away from Christian duty before the insidious temptations which surrounded them.

It has all along been a most serious difficulty in the Red Land that there are no local markets for labour, and no industries which can absorb the more intelligent lads. There is only one vocation, and this is teaching. A very few others have also learned building, carpentry and allied industries, but for the great bulk of the population the only avenue to wage-earning is in other lands.

At first Blantyre and the Shire Highlands took all the labour that was willing to go there. But as the Rhodesian mines and farms developed, Nyasaland boys began to find their way there ; and, when they returned with gold instead of silver, with boxes laden with old European clothing and tin ware, instead of little bundles of Manchester cloth, with hats on their heads and marvellous military boots on their feet, streams of ambitious youths began to flow south.

Had Nyasaland been a legitimate recruiting ground for the Labour Bureau, the terrible sufferings which these travellers endured on the long journey south might have been mitigated, and their due return organised. But the Nyasaland boys had all to wander south independently of any shepherding by a wealthy organisation. Many died ; others waited on year after year unable to save enough to justify their return, and others disappeared, having sunk into a morass of evil conduct from which they could not extricate themselves.

While the conditions of travel and of labour were at their worst, I spoke to Daniel one day about the losses to village life. " Yes, sir," he said, "there is a more deadly war to-day than our Abangoni raiding. It is at the mines in South Africa."

One after another of Daniel's friends went south, some to return and share their goods with him, after the fashion of the real communism of the people. While they were abroad, he cared for their relatives and families. When they returned, they were not

Tempting Offers

unmindful. Others again entrusted him with their savings, sending money orders for him to cash, and keep the money against their return. This banking transaction yielded no interest. No ledger fee or other reward was given to Daniel for his trouble. He had the anxiety of keeping the money and of distributing according to instructions what sums were to be given to wife and parents. Yet all this was done without a grudge, and without hope of reward, out of that social loyalty which one member of an African society feels towards another.

Chapter XXI

A VILLAGE FLITTING

TO A NEW DISTRICT BECOMES NECESSARY FOR REASONS
WHICH ARE DETAILED, AND WHILE IT IS IN
PROGRESS THE RED LAND IS ANNEXED BY
THE BRITISH GOVERNMENT

FOR over fifteen years the Hoho villagers had
been cultivating in the valley of the Kasitu.
That was a long time for Abangoni to be
settled at one place. They had meanwhile successfully deforested the whole of that neighbourhood,
ruined the productiveness of the soil, and filled the
rivers and marshes with sand, so that little water was
to be seen there save in the rainy season. Now it was
time to move out into the untenanted woods that lay
to the south, and open fresh fields.

During their long sojourn at the Kasitu each
village had shifted its site many times. Five years
made a hut venerable, but not beautiful. In five
years a village was tottering to decay and becoming
so full of unpleasant things that " home " ceased to
speak of quiet and comfort.

First there was the unhappy custom of the Abangoni of burying their dead within the village, before
the door of the home. In five years a village of two
hundred inhabitants had very many birth rejoicings,
but, alas! too many wailings for death; so that
among the crowded cluster of huts there lay little

A Village Flitting

heaps of heavy stones, covered with earth and weeds, where members of the village lay buried. The constant sight of these graves was depressing. The Christians in the Hoho villages were now burying their dead with Christian worship in a little plot of ground set apart. But their custom was not the custom of all, and the Christians were still a small minority in each community. By Christians and heathen alike the ancient custom of burying a headman beside his cattle-kraal was still retained.

Again, the white ants were very voracious. The mud with which the walls of the huts were plastered provided capital tunnels through which they could reach the poles which held the house together, and in five years they could eat up every stick in the wall that was at all appetising. Then the grass on the roof rotted with rain and sun, and the grass on the eaves was so convenient for any housewife who wanted a little torch when she searched for a mislaid article in the night, or who was in a hurry to make her smouldering log burst into flame, that the eaves were gradually bared of all the grass that made them effective.

And, chiefly, there were many biting things that found refuge in the daytime up in the grass roofs, in little holes of the wall, and within the cluster of pots in the darkest corner of the hut, and came out when all was still to make their meal on the blood of the sleeping inhabitants. In five years' time their numbers became legion.

For these reasons the people perforce changed the site of their homes from time to time and built new ones.

Daniel in his own village, and some of his brothers in theirs, were among the first to erect large, square houses. They were the better able to do this because

A Village Flitting

one of the younger brothers had been trained as a carpenter. He made doors for them, and shuttered windows which could open and let light and air into the rooms. It was a long and expensive job to build such a house, and when one was finished the owner was in no hurry to move off to a new site and build another. Consequently, these villages remained longer in one place, and more care was taken by the people who were compelled to stay to keep their houses in repair.

Yet the primitive huts could not stand for ever, and removal must take place. More serious was the fact that the fields were not producing sufficient for the year's need of the families, and locusts were covering them every year and eating up the young maize.

Out of this famine and discomfort groups of people were flitting away and building in the lands to the south which had not been occupied for a generation or two. The indiscriminate scattering was becoming so general that the people were no longer under the control of their chiefs ; therefore it was suggested that a general migration of the southern section of the tribe should take place, chiefs and people going together.

With this movement my own station at Hora was carried south, and a new one was built in the heart of the lands that were being occupied. The Hoho people who had been our near neighbours at Hora passed on to high, wooded lands twenty miles south-east of our new settlement, and there Daniel built his own village.

The change of residence to a cooler country was good for him, for the inherent delicacy of his constitution was revealing itself in repeated illnesses.

A Village Flitting

Shortly before the migration he had an attack of pneumonia. My wife was called in as his doctor, and, when she first visited him, found his house full of people waiting for his death. He was very weak, and it seemed as if he had not much longer to live. In the expectation of death he gave his charges about his wife and children and property, and then called on the weeping friends to yield themselves to God. Panting in his weakness he urged with the earnestness of a dying man that they follow his Saviour, and then led in the singing of a hymn. But this sickness was not unto death, and he slowly recovered from it.

Next year, 1902, the migration took place, and shortly afterwards the British Government formally took over the administration of the Abangoni. This latter great event was necessitated by the increasing complication of intertribal relations and by the coming and going of many Europeans. It was effected by the Governor himself during a short visit, quietly and without any demonstration of force. When the annexation was completed the Governor gave all the credit to the mission for the great dramatic success which attended his visit.

No one rejoiced more over the establishment of strong and righteous rule by the Europeans than did Daniel. He knew from bitter experience how impossible it was to restrain any lawless white man who might come among them, and he was very well aware that the new chiefs, as well as the old ones, had no authority over their own people because they could not use the terror of the spear ; that many of them were taking bribes, and favouring their friends in judging cases, and that misrule was on the increase.

Daniel was not present at the great " indaba " when the Governor met the chiefs. Indeed, he and his

A Village Flitting

family had suffered so much for their share in the settling of the Europeans in the Red Land that he determined that the present momentous change should take place without his being too closely identified with it. What was to happen in the future was unknown, but he could foresee that many would resent a justice that could not be bribed, punishments that fell on the guilty whether they were great chiefs or unprotected slaves, and, above all, the taxation which in time must follow administration.

During this critical period he remained in his village and was much in prayer. Two or three days after the annexation I called on him on my way back to my own station, and reported on the happy and peaceful result of the " indaba." Then he broke into praise and thankfulness to God, Whose guiding Hand he recognised in the whole transaction.

Daniel and his brothers now began to settle in the new territory of which they had taken possession. It was a wide, tree-covered, hilly country near the sources of the Dwambazi River which flowed to the Lake. The soil was very rich and had never been occupied before. It was so high, and so near the open grass-lands, that very cold winds blew for some months in the year and thick mists hung over it. There was room there for all, and the richest promise of great maize crops. Many villages, therefore, which had years before left the neighbourhood of the Hoho group, returned from the valleys in which they had settled, and again clustered near the village of their chief.

Unfortunately the cattle did not prosper. They were unaccustomed to the cold, and the grass was rank. But Daniel's optimism believed that in a year or so his estate would turn out to be a first-class cattle-country.

A Village Flitting

With abundance of good timber near at hand and with some experience behind them, the head-men proceeded to found villages greatly superior to the old ones in the Kasitu Valley. More room was allowed between the huts, which were also of a more substantial order. Daniel and his brothers were ambitious, too, to try to grow a greater variety of food-stuffs. Bananas were carried away from the mission garden, orange and lemon seedlings, wheat, potatoes, and other foreign plants. It was always a delight to visit this good land, enjoy the abundant hospitality of the people, and see the big fields of dark, waving maize and the barns filled with food, which was so much more than would be required by the family that some improvident folk were leaving maize in the fields unreaped, as there was already sufficient in the stores.

But, in spite of the constant praise of this excellent land, there were two disturbing factors. One was that the cattle were dying ; and the other was that villagers who had set distance between themselves and others, because of old quarrels, had comes together again still remembering their feuds. Again and again the enmities of the past found new irritations and disturbed the friendly spirit that should have obtained.

This led Daniel and his younger brother, Yobe, one of the *indunas*, to hive off again and seek quarters where they would have peace. Thirty miles farther south they selected a very rich valley where the cold certainly would not trouble them, and where there was every promise of splendid harvests. That was their final migration ; for in a few years the unoccupied land became covered with new settlers, and then the Government proceeded to mark out the boundaries within which the people must abide.

A Village Flitting

Here Daniel built a much more ambitious village, and a fine square house for himself. Here he planted his fruit trees and saw them prosper, his wheat and potatoes and whatever seeds he could get with which to experiment. And here he found unusual opportunity for every kind of ambition in social progress.

Chapter XXII

THE EVANGELIST

ONE result of the great migration of the people was that it brought a vast number of villages into close contact with the new station at Loudon, and at the same time broke down barriers of suspicion which had made many unwilling to receive the teachers. The presence of the British Government in the land had created, in the eyes of the ignorant, an unknown menace to the old isolation, and head-men were eager to have a teacher near at hand for advice and protection, when police or others bearing messages from the magistrate should come to them.

In time we were inundated with requests for teachers. Although these could only be answered gradually, our schools were increasing too rapidly. We decided, therefore, to appoint from among our most tested teachers a number of evangelists who would stimulate the religious service of the schools, and who would travel constantly in couples, preaching the Word to the people who had no regular instruction. Daniel was one of these first evangelists. His great friend, Andrew Mkochi, was another, and his younger brother, Simon, yet another. There were six in all, and all of them were elders of the church.

At intervals of six weeks or two months they came

The Evangelist

to Loudon and spent a week with me, while I led them
through regular teaching in the New Testament, the
Pilgrim's Progress and other books. Between these
visits to me they travelled, two and two, through all
the district, spending a day or two at each school,
helping the teachers, visiting the Christians in their
homes and praying with the sick. They passed
through the unoccupied villages, holding services and
sitting with the people, talking to them of their
evangel.

Usually they were received with much courtesy
and the people listened eagerly to their message, but
Andrew and Daniel had a very wide, sparsely occupied
territory for their field and frequently found fear and
resentment of their work. It took all their tact and
courage to disarm the cloudy suspicion and explain
for what they came.

One day they approached the village of a great
witch-doctor whose reputation and wealth depended
on keeping the teachers away. He heard that they
were coming, for they had been moving slowly in his
direction from village to village, and he determined
to turn them back with the fearsomeness of his occult
powers. Donning all the wild regalia of the full-
blown witch-doctor he lay in wait for them by the
path. Then suddenly the awful figure of the expert
in magic rose before them, feathers and bladders and
ribbons on his head; bones and strips of skin about
his neck; horns filled with magic across his chest;
zebra tails and other oddments fluttering in his hands.
With a soul-moving growl he began to dance and point
his magic stick at the evangelists.

But Daniel knew all about it, and he stood on the
path and laughed. The wilder the prancing of the
doctor grew, the more Daniel laughed, and then he

cried to the exhausted magician, " I have no fear of your horns, nor of any witch-doctor. God alone I fear."

Away slunk the defeated doctor and shut himself up in his hut, knowing that his day was over. But not many months went past before a request came from him that he might have a school and teachers. When I went there next I found his own stalwart sons the leaders and brightest pupils in the school.

Not long after this Daniel came to the village of Suku, then an old man with a considerable population about him and kraals well stocked with cattle. Andrew had been left behind at another village to conduct a funeral service over a little child. Daniel sat down and talked a little with the village people, who told him that old Suku was lying very ill in his hut. When the preaching which followed soon after was finished, Daniel engaged in prayer and asked for Suku's recovery.

Now although it was a man like themselves who was speaking, only a little of what he had to say was understood, for a great prejudice distorted his words. One thing the people had heard—that Daniel had prayed to God for Suku, mentioning his name. This alarmed them, and they muttered to one another, " Our father Suku will die. The teacher has prayed to God, and He is the bringer of death."

Daniel, however, paying no attention to these ignorant fears, went to Suku's hut and, after some talk with him, prayed by his bedside that he might recover.

Next day Andrew arrived. Then the alarm of the villagers was doubled, for they said, " He has called another teacher to help his prayers."

The two evangelists visited Suku together, and

tried to explain to him that they were God's servants and the messengers of everlasting life. Then they prayed over him that God would heal his sickness.

From that time the old man began to recover rapidly and soon was out and about, and his people's fears were turned to rejoicings. Now that he had found how saving were the prayers of the evangelists nothing would satisfy him but that he also should have teachers, and he sent a little deputation to Loudon to ask this favour.

Shortly afterwards my wife and I called at his village, bringing the teachers with us. Great was our welcome. The village was all swept and tidied that it might be worthy our coming. A fine fat bull was given us that our men might have food to eat, and the school was opened with much enthusiasm.

Every visit back to the kindly old gentleman was embarrassing in its hospitality. The next time I went there he gave me a cow to be wife to the bull of the previous welcome, and, though I hated the idea of slaughtering it, he insisted that one must eat, and this was only " a little fowl " he had given us.

The order of evangelists proved so useful and timely that the Mission Council took it in hand and a regular course of instruction was arranged at the Institution. This necessitated that the evangelists should be accepted by Presbytery and should go up to the Institution for training for five months every year.

At last Daniel's long ambition was to be gratified to some extent, and he became a student at the Institution. Eagerly he drank in his lessons on the Bible, and Doctrine, and Church History, and Experimental Religion, and when he came back for the long seven months' vacation and returned to the practical work

The Evangelist

of the evangelist his sermons were enriched by many a reference to doctors of the Church and to the stories of the early history of Christianity.

When the three years were over, he received the certificate of the Presbytery and, with the others, became an accredited evangelist of the native Church, who also paid him his salary.

The numbers of the Christians continued to increase and the area for which our station was responsible to expand. Then it became necessary to divide the Church into several districts or parishes, each more or less self-contained. The Loudon area, which comprised a diocese of about twelve thousand square miles, was divided into eight congregations, each of which will, in time, have its native minister, but until we should be able to provide them with ordained men the evangelists acted as pastors of the congregation under pretty close supervision.

Daniel was one of those under-shepherds. He had by this time many years of experience in teaching, had taken his certificate as an evangelist, had been an elder of the Church from the day when elders were first elected, and all the time had grown in staid responsibility and in tireless service for the Kingdom. His judgment had matured, and men looked to him as one of the fathers of the Church.

Behold him now, presiding over his monthly meeting of elders and deacons. He sits at the table in a central school, somewhat shabbily dressed in clothes one or two sizes too big for his slight frame. On his nose lies a pair of steel-rimmed spectacles which needs to be pushed up nearer his eyes every now and then. A well-worn Zulu Bible is in front of him. Between the pages are many loose leaves, somewhat yellowed by the smoke of hut fires and scribbled over with

The Evangelist

sermon notes and names of people. He has already welcomed his dozen leaders with a hearty smile and shake of the hand, and has laid his pencil and minute-book before him.

With a sharp movement he rises and says, " Let us pray," and for a few moments he addresses God in words living with faith and feeling, as he constitutes the sub-session meeting.

Then the subdued elders and he get to business. First there are little sums of money, the monthly contributions of the members, to be handed over by the deacons, and these are painfully counted out with his twisted fingers and each sum is entered in his minute-book. Then the elders bring under review cases of discipline, or restoration, or problems of ethics and marriage. Daniel is a keen cross-examiner. He bores his way to the bottom of every case, remembers all past references to it and has first-hand knowledge of the circumstances under discussion. After these cases have been thoroughly considered, a short summary is written into his minute-book, to be presented to the larger session-meeting when the Moderator—or " Modulator " as some elders will pronounce it—is present. It is a slow business entering all this, for Daniel is a cramped, poor writer.

Next he speaks to the elders about arrangements for a mission or convention he is going to hold. All the details are discussed and the speakers fixed. Throughout the talk Daniel's eyes have been flashing inspiration. He has a kindly way of calling his elders " brothers," which makes them feel that they are one with him in all the work to be done. And then with fervent prayer, led by two or three of the " brothers," the session-meeting is closed.

181

The Evangelist

The influence that he and other evangelists had over their people was not acquired by any fictitious authority of office, but by hard service. They travelled constantly, usually accompanied by a boy who carried their blanket and " Sunday clothes " and Bible. In every village they preached. By the wayside they talked with travellers. At the kraal gate they sat with the villagers and listened to all the gossip of the idlers. By the fireside they worshipped with the groups who resorted to their hut for help. They knew individually every person in their field and all his family history, and not a few of the leaders of the Church were their own children in the faith.

But deeper than their service was the testimony of their character. What they were day by day in their own villages and families was public property. And the influence and power of the evangelists depended, not a little, on what was known and said of them by their fellow-citizens.

Chapter XXIII

PERILS OF THE WAY

ARE SUGGESTED BY WHAT BEFELL DANIEL DURING HIS
MANY JOURNEYS, AND BY THE MURDER
OF A FELLOW-EVANGELIST

THE districts of which Daniel was in charge from time to time were wide and wild. At one place numerous villages clustered together; then would follow a long reach of bush or tree-land without inhabitant. Sometimes where water was scarce a single small village would be found in a clearing of the trees, and then for miles stretched woods through which wild beasts roamed, but where no village was visible.

Among these populated centres and desolate reaches, Daniel, with a young boy as his companion, travelled continuously, for we had now ceased to send the evangelists in couples. The fatigue of such incessant work was great, and Daniel was never a robust man. Too often he was prostrated with severe illnesses, and twice we almost despaired of his life. But no thought of himself hindered him from the greatest fatigues in the service of the Kingdom, and no terrors of men or beasts made him turn aside from a single journey.

One day he was crossing the hills in a wild part of the country, all alone. Here the face of the land is covered with a thick scrub that grows over deserted gardens, and the villages lay very far apart. He had not been well when he started, and, as the day advanced, his fever increased until at length he could go no farther. So he turned aside, and, rolling his blanket about him, lay down to sleep, that after rest he might continue his journey. The deep sleep into which Africans so easily fall at any moment and in any place laid hold of him. When he wakened he found to his horror that the sun had gone down and the night was rapidly approaching. He jumped to his feet and, rolling up his blanket, started off as fast as he could walk for the nearest village. But it was miles away, and the night was black as pitch and the bush full of terrors.

Fully expecting to meet a lion or a leopard at any minute, stumbling along the narrow track, he kept his mind in perfect peace, trusting in God. At last, far into the night, he arrived safely among human habitations. There was no doubt in his mind that God had been all about him and had brought him through, and he was no sooner in assured safety than he gave public thanks for God's keeping.

Sometimes, not from lack of goodwill but from sheer inability, the people could not provide him with what was necessary for comfort. The huts might be old and in disrepair. He would try the one which was given him as guest-room, but the night would not have gone far before he would be forced by the numerous other and very wakeful inhabitants to turn out and sleep in the open air.

In the course of his travels he arrived in a village which was wholly given over to beer drinking. They had been favoured with a particularly good harvest of the little millet grain with which they prepared their heady beer. Daniel found the village full of

A NATIVE BRIDGE CROSSING THE RUMPI

INSTITUTION QUARRY

strangers, who had gathered for a great carousal. For some days the feast had been in progress and no food had been prepared except huge pots of beer. The drink has excellent food properties, being not unlike a very thin gruel which has fermented.

The people hospitably offered him as much of their intoxicating food as he would take, but Daniel was now an abstainer and would take none. Unfortunately there was nothing else in the village to give him, and that night he slept supperless. All next day he was busy with his evangelist's work among a people too sodden with beer to appreciate his message, and all that day he passed fasting.

Next morning he started off with his young companion to cross the long uninhabited land that lay before him. Faint with hunger, he soon found himself unable to proceed farther, and said to his companion, " Let us pray to God." In the wood they knelt down together, and Daniel spoke to God of Elijah His servant, whom He had fed by the ravens, and of the birds which the Father feeds, and trusted that much more would He feed His servants who were on His errands.

When he rose from his knees he looked about him to see what answer God had given, and spied not far off among the bushes a sacred *msoro* tree, and hanging among its branches a goodly bunch of maize, which some worshipper had placed there as an offering to his god or ancestral spirit.

Daniel felt no more compunction about taking it than did David when he took the shew-bread. His companion soon struck up a fire by friction and in a short time they were merrily roasting the maize over a good blaze. I doubt not that one day the unknown worshipper came back to that sacred tree and, seeing that his offering had gone, concluded that his god had accepted the gift and had shown himself friendly. Perhaps his deduction was right.

As for the evangelist, there was no doubt in his mind that the Heavenly Father had caused that maize to be placed there to feed His fainting servants. In the strength of this divine food he continued his journey until he arrived at his destination. There the people cooked maize porridge for him, killed a fowl, and stewed it in a pot to be relish for his porridge. So he ate and gave thanks.

We never cared to let the evangelists attempt to tour their districts alone, as they sometimes did for economy's sake, or for lack of proper arrangements. Unfortunately we were to receive a most tragic lesson on the danger that might lie in wait for the lonely traveller.

One of our most tireless and enthusiastic men was called Andrew Kalemba. He had finished his theological studies for the ministry, but we had not proceeded to ordain him, as he was the victim of a strange drowsiness which overtook him at all seasons and greatly diminished the respect with which people regarded him. He invariably dropped off to sleep in church during the sermon, which is not peculiar or to be wondered at. But, should he sit down in school and wait for a little to see what was being done, he fell asleep straightway, to the amusement of the pupils. He slept through session-meetings, when we required all his attention for the discussion of a difficult case. I have even seen him go to sleep as he stood ringing the church bell.

To others this was very funny, but for him it was

Perils of the Way

painful and humiliating. For there was no one on the whole staff so passionately in earnest, so constant and faithful in his service. When preaching his appeal became so tremendous that I have seen him dancing out his call to men, and he had the pleasant originality of sometimes bursting into song in the midst of his sermon, singing his own hymn to his own music to illustrate his theme. His prayerfulness was great. Many a time he spent the night alone in the woods praying for his people.

I had called the evangelists to Loudon to meet me a day or two before the annual Convention, and all came but Kalemba. By and by the people from his villages arrived and told us that he had started before them, travelling alone as he often did.

Days passed and no word was heard of him. So we sent out searchers, fearing that some evil had befallen him. A week or so afterwards his body, stripped of all its clothing, was found in a pool near the Government station. No one could account for his death until some weeks had elapsed, when a teacher reported that two men had tried to sell Kalemba's books and clothes to him. These men were arrested, and bit by bit the story was pieced together.

The two men had been travelling along the Government road, and quite near the station had seen Kalemba sitting beneath a tree sound asleep. They knocked him on the head, stripped him of his clothes, and threw his body into the pool, and went off, carrying away his books and clothing.

The evidence seemed to be very conclusive, and they were both condemned by the magistrate to be hanged. But there was some flaw in the chain of evidence, and the judge at headquarters, who reviewed

Perils of the Way

it, pronounced the case "not proven," so they were released.

They are both ordinary villagers, not to be distinguished from the other men who talk with them at the kraal gate by any peculiar passion or stinging remorse. They still laugh with them, and live with them, and get drunk with them. No fellow-villager shuns them or thinks differently of them, though everyone knows they are murderers.

Yet one must not think that this was not a horrible and unusual thing for the people to hear of, and that men of other villages did not express their detestation of so foul a murder.

Human beings, however, were not nearly so dangerous as wild beasts, and no one knew where these latter might be lurking. Part of the district which Daniel had under his care at one time was often plagued with leopards, and sometimes with lions, and he had his adventures. He was coming to meet me at a central school one day, and he had left his village alone and was hurrying to be in time for my arrival. As he passed along the edge of a stream he noticed a little bird that was behaving in an eccentric way on a large tree which stood amid a clump of tall grass and shrubbery. The bird fluttered from branch to branch, and seemed to wish to come to ground, but there was something there that kept it from landing. Daniel said to himself that either a snake or leopard must be lying in the cover, and he approached very carefully, for the path ran along the fringe of the shrubs.

Just as he came near to the tree a leopard rose to its feet and faced him with an angry cry. Daniel was thoroughly startled, but he stood still and defied the brute, shouting his old war-cry, "Hau! Hau!"

Perils of the Way

Evidently his firm defiance was too much for the leopard, for instead of springing on him it leapt aside into the thicket and disappeared. But the little man got a real fright, and ran every step of the way to the school, where he arrived panting and excited.

Chapter XXIV

THE PREACHER

THAT DANIEL WAS BEFORE AND AFTER HIS THEOLOGICAL
TRAINING IS DESCRIBED IN TWO PICTURES
OF HIM AT WORK

WITH the development of the native Church the Livingstonia Mission had found it necessary to prepare a native ministry. By-and-by three men who had gone through prolonged experience as teachers, and then had taken the full normal course at the Institution and afterwards a few years in theology, were ordained to the ministry.

It was now proposed that a modified course should be framed which should carry some of the tested evangelists forward to the full ministry, and, when names like those of Daniel and Andrew, his friend, were suggested, the Mission Council was heartily in favour of the proposal.

Years before both lads had definitely dedicated themselves to the service of the Kingdom. They had been discussing together their past work and the fifteen years during which they had served the mission. Tempting offers had been put before each of them to go into more highly paid employment, and had been rejected, and they said to one another, " God has put great honour on us in calling us to serve Him. He has served us all the days of our life,

The Preacher

and it is well that we give ourselves to His service ;
and in this service let us die."

When the elders, then, proposed to submit the
names of these two honoured evangelists to the
Presbytery as possible students for the ministry they
were but opening a way by which they both might
more fully complete the dedication of their lives.

Daniel and Andrew then returned to the Institution for further training. In 1915 they both completed their course of study and were licensed by the
Presbytery to be preachers of the Word. That day
was a very great one for them. Only three questions
were asked : " What is your motive in seeking to be
a minister of the Church ? What do you consider
to be the chief work of a minister ? What do you
recognise to be the great doctrines you desire to
preach ? " Of these questions they had had timely
notice, and both prepared and wrote out with great
care the replies that they should give in public.

Andrew answered calmly and reasonably, not
without great nervousness and feeling. Daniel stood
beside his handsome and stalwart friend, a delicate,
intense man with a slight figure, and spoke with a
great conviction ringing in his voice. He centred
much around the Cross in his statement, and the
possibility of fellowship with God, and through all
the ring of sincerity and personal experience was
audible.

Now he returned to the practical work of the
ministry to fulfil a two years' probation before he
should be ordained. The work given to him was just
what he had already been doing as an evangelist, but
he was equipped with maturer experience, some
knowledge of the relation of his faith to the past
and to the Catholic Church, and a surer interpreta-

The Preacher

tion of the Bible. Sometimes I had the privilege
of hearing him preach in the Loudon church, and
then, of course, he gave us his very best. At first
I feared that the training at the Institution had
spoiled his natural gifts of oratory. For he prepared
his sermons carefully, and carried with him into the
pulpit full notes which he rather slavishly followed.
His attractive naturalness was crushed by his con-
scientious efforts to adhere to the formal exposition
of his subject, and his illustrations, instead of being
drawn from the familiar things of everyday life and
the old history of the tribe, were unearthed from
lectures he had heard on Church History and from
the puzzling incidents of European life. Gradually
he recovered his freedom, and again we could see
the little eager man flashing and dancing in his zeal
to make his arrows sharp and to send them home
when he shot.

I shall give two sketches of our preacher. One is
drawn from the days before he had gone for his
special training to the Institution, the other from the
time when he was a " probationer " of the Church.

The first scene was during one of the annual conventions at Ekwendeni. Meetings were held all day
long outside the church, for the multitudes were too
great to be accommodated within the building. The
preachers spoke from a raised platform set against
the wall of the church. The full diets in the daylight
only seemed to sharpen the appetites of the people
for more, so they arranged that they should meet
again at night, when some of the native elders should
address them.

One night, along with Dr. Elmslie, our host, we
wandered round in the dark to look at the congregation that had assembled. An indistinct mass of

The Preacher

humanity stretched out before us, and far away on the platform, standing in the light of a single lamp on the table, Daniel was in full swing with his sermon.

He had left his coat at his sleeping booth, and stood in his ill-fitting shirt and trousers, an old pair of braces showing up very distinctly, and giving him a curiously " working " appearance that was scarcely ecclesiastical. He was pouring forth a warm commendation of the Lord Jesus as an efficient Saviour for all types of sin. " In the doctor's dispensary," he was saying, " there are rows and rows of bottles. This bottle has medicine which will stop your cough, and this other will heal your ulcers, and this other will relieve your fever. The Great Physician, too, has a bottle for every kind of disease of the soul. O drunkard, whom beer has bound hand and foot, Jesus has medicine which will save you from the love of drink. I have drunk this medicine and it has healed me. O wild and passionate one, whose hands have been red with blood, Jesus has a bottle which will make you gentle as a child and tame your ungoverned temper. O adulterer, whose sins have roused hatred and broken up villages, Jesus has a bottle that will make you pure and chaste." Thus he went on, pouring out knowledge of the adaptability of the Saviour for every type of sinner in the audience.

When we turned aside to go back to the house we left the little preacher still uttering the passionate appeals of his ardent soul, restlessly moving up and down the platform, his hands waving in never-ending but graceful movement, and his voice wooing and convincing.

Another scene was on a Wednesday afternoon at the mid-week prayer meeting at Loudon. Daniel

The Preacher

had come in from one of his long tours to report on his district, and I had asked him to speak. He agreed with great alacrity, and gave us one of his exact and carefully prepared expositions, which were the result of his training at the Institution.

This day he was speaking of Christ coming to the disciples on the water, and how they were afraid at first, but, after they knew Him, joyfully received Him into the boat. He gave us this idyll of native life as an illustration.

A young wife was sitting by herself in her hut. Years before her husband had gone to the mines in Southern Rhodesia to work, and had not returned. How she missed him as the weary months passed! The children were growing up and she had no one to help her with their training. Sorrows had met her again and again, and she longed for her husband's support. Often she sought the strength and sympathy that his companionship alone could give her, and longed to tell him about all the interests of her life.

As he opened up the possibilities of companionship between man and wife we sat amazed, looking in at a window that had been opened, and seeing a sweet, attractive picture of the relations that sometimes existed between an African man and wife which is seldom given to a European to see. But the most wonderful part was to look down on the audience and watch the women's fascination. Their eyes were following him with a wistful tenderness and tears were gathering in some.

Then he went on to tell how, one night, as the woman sat in her loneliness there came a knocking at the reed door. She trembled to hear it. Who was this standing without at this late hour? Was

The Preacher

it some evil man with wicked thoughts? She sat
silent, making no answer, and the knocking was renewed. Fearful and trembling, she cried at last,
"Who is there?"

A voice answered, "It is I."

At first it struck her with terror, for she could not
believe her ears, and she cried again, "Who are
you?"

Then his voice answered, her own husband's, no
doubt about it. How quickly she rose, and with
hands that trembled with excitement undid the
door and welcomed her husband back again. Then,
when he sat down with her once more upon the
mat, she knew that she had him all to herself. What
multitudes of things she had to tell him, and how
all the burdens rolled from her and her life became
fresh and joyful again!

Of course, our preacher did not always find so happy
illustrations or touch the feelings of his audience so
deeply. Sometimes he rose to great heights of suggestion and appeal, and at other times was laboured
and commonplace. His emotional nature quickly
responded to the atmosphere in which he was speaking, and sometimes there was a wealth of illustration
which the people could well understand, a naturalness of diction, and, with all, a tender appeal which
revealed how far he had moved from the old fiery
denunciation by which he used to try to waken the
heathen.

The sick and the inquirers found in him a sympathy
which knit them to their teacher. He was brave in
his faith by the sick-bed, and many a time prayed
definitely for healing there and then, rousing the
faith of a despondent patient by his own buoyant
faith. In his daily diary of travel and work he care-

The Preacher

fully recorded the answers to these prayers for the sick and his praise to God, the Healer.

His band of elders found him to be the wisest of judges. How he wormed himself into the very heart of a case, ignored the irrelevancies and discovered the truth in spite of all efforts to hide it! How safe he was from allowing judgments to be pronounced when only one side of the case had been heard! And how he saved his legalistically inclined fellow-elders from harsh penalties and hard attitudes towards the sinner with whom they had to do!

Up and down his wide district he held continual missions for the deepening of the spiritual life of the Church and to utter more insistently the call to repentance. His preaching was attractive enough to draw large congregations, but no rabble was allowed to spoil the religious atmosphere of the gatherings. His sternness with giddy girls and wanton lads who would have ruined his great assemblies sent them away frightened and subdued.

Chapter XXV

HIS CHARACTER

AS A HUSBAND AND FATHER, WITH THE TRAGEDY OF HIS
DAUGHTER'S DEATH, AND AS A HOSPITABLE AND
COURTEOUS GENTLEMAN, IS ILLUSTRATED,
CLOSING WITH A STORY OF SPORTIVE
LION CUBS

THE night after Daniel had the adventure with the leopard (Chap. XXIII) we spent together in the guest-room of the teacher's house. The fire burned brightly in the middle of the floor, and three or four of us sat about on mats beside the fire talking. The snuff-box was passed round again and again, and Daniel, who was still excited with his adventure of the morning, was in great form.

I had led the conversation on to home life and suggested that, with their system of marriage, it was not often that there was true companionship between husband and wife, and that the women were used too much as mere slaves of the men. But Daniel would not have it at all. He could give instances of real affection between a married pair which showed itself in most gentle consideration for one another. And then he began to tell about his own wife, and the patient, loving care she showed him in time of sickness. One story he told of her long devotion to him when he was very ill, and how she never left his side day or night, watching every turn and moan he made, ready at any moment to do some little kindness to ease his distress. This, he thought, was an unanswerable proof of the self-sacrificing devotion that sometimes bound wife to husband.

Indeed, Daniel had moulded his wife by his own tender affection for her. One admired his treatment of his sons, vivacious, manly little fellows, whom he guided with a strictness that was not resented by them, for it was governed by a very evident pride and affection. Their natural place when he sat in his house in friendly talk was by his side, cuddling in to him. Day by day, when he was at home, he talked to them of the things of the Kingdom and encouraged them in their efforts to learn. All his soul was bound up in his youngest daughter, who was the joy of her father's eyes. It was his love to his eldest son that had led him into the faith of Christ, and it was the tragedy of his youngest daughter that was the most terrible trial of his life.

One day we were sitting with the elders at Loudon, discussing Church matters. About fifty of these leaders were present, and Daniel was there, sitting along with his friend Andrew, leading our counsels. I had been talking about some phase of work to which I was trying to give an inspiring lead when a stranger entered the room and whispered something to Daniel. He immediately rose and went out with him. A minute or two afterwards a voice whispered tremblingly at my back, " Good-bye, sir, I am going home."

I looked round and there saw Daniel. He was suddenly shrivelled up and was shaking from head to foot.

" What's wrong, Daniel ? " I asked in the utmost concern.

His Character

"I have just heard that my youngest daughter has been killed," he whispered.

"Oh, Daniel!" was all I could answer.

But Andrew had seen all, and was up in a moment. Taking Daniel by the hand he led him into another room. I followed, and the elders sat silently with alarmed faces. When I entered the next room Andrew was sitting with his arms about his friend, and then the story, as the messenger had told it, was repeated.

A little niece of Daniel's wife had been adopted into his house, much against his will. He thought her a wilful and badly trained girl whose presence would be an evil to his own family, but his wife had pressed the matter so far that at last he yielded. Two days before his niece and youngest daughter were playing together in the village, and the niece, who had a long bamboo in her hand, struck her little cousin over the spleen and she fell down dead. It was all the result of an accident, but it had been immediately fatal.

Daniel was forty miles from home, and he started off at once, his brother Yobe and Andrew accompanying him. It was an anxious journey, for poor Daniel had completely collapsed. He had no words but a continual moan, "My child! my child!"

When they arrived home they found the whole community in great excitement. Some were demanding the death of the niece, or the heaviest possible payments by the relatives; others were silent in terror before the calamity that had befallen them. But as soon as Daniel had heard the story he arranged for the burial and emphatically declared that no harm was to be done to his little niece, but she was to be sent back to her own village.

His Character

He had taken the Christian line, but his own soul was bowed down to the dust. For two days after the funeral he remained in the deepest dejection. He refused to taste food, and seemed unable to rest or sleep. On the fourth day Andrew brought him a dish of pleasant food, but he would not touch it. Then Andrew said with great firmness, " Well, if you will not eat, neither will I. I will starve along with you."

Suddenly the folly of the situation broke on Daniel, and with a wan smile he looked on his friend's face and said, " Let us eat."

The two ate together, and from that time some quiet and comfort began to come to the broken parent. He soon became aware that his wife was far more seriously affected than he was. For her mind was oppressed with the sense that she had insisted on her niece's presence in the family in spite of her husband's protests. Now she was sitting in unmitigated grief, blaming herself for all that had happened. Daniel had, then, to rouse himself to comfort her, and for weeks after he tried every artifice to soften the pain that was eating into her soul.

Hospitality, one of the great virtues of the early Church, was also one of Daniel's shining characteristics. In civilised lands travellers may enter an eating-house and buy what they require for their refreshment and hire rooms in inns where they may rest and sleep. The feeding of the hungry has become a profitable profession, and hospitality is only the adjunct of sociable intercourse. But in Africa there are neither hotels nor eating-houses. The traveller depends on the friendliness of the people for a house to sleep in and a mat on which he may lie. Unless he carries his provisions with him he

THE BEGINNING OF A VILLAGE SCHOOL

A MODERN NATIVE HOUSE

This is a high-class house belonging to a native Christian. It contains three rooms,
fire-places with chimneys, and windows. It is built of mud and poles, and thatched
with grass. Only the chimneys and fire-place and the outer rim of the verandah
have bricks.

can eat only when people invite him to partake
with them.

Where streams of carriers and other travellers are
always passing no one now expects this hospitality.
The stranger either carries the food he requires for
his journey, or buys meal at high prices from the
villagers who happen to have some prepared. Otherwise the drain on the resources of those who live
near the trade routes would become impossible.

Happily in the other districts which have not been
so inundated there still exists large opportunity to
preserve the old-world hospitality to strangers. I
have more than once heard my men discussing the
various receptions they have had on our constant
tours. Here the people were churlish; would not
sell their food; had only filthy, " biting " huts for
them when they asked for a place in which they might
sleep. There the people were friendly; bringing
presents of meal; cooking dishes of porridge; providing a good house and mats on which they might
lie. To the carriers there was no better measure of
virtue and of vice than one's treatment of strangers.

When the discussions went on I would find Daniel's
name mentioned as an example of what hospitality
should be. Fortunately there was always plenty of
food in his barns, and his people had been trained
to treat the stranger kindly. His connections were
immense. He was related in various ways to numerous
people all over the tribe. He had been evangelist
and teacher to thousands of folk, and when he moved
about among their villages they fed him and housed
him.

Now when they in turn were travelling they would
enter his village to greet him and rest there for the
night. When they came they knew well that he would

be ready to give them water to drink, food to eat, and a mat to sleep on beside a friendly fire. It was a great grace, fulfilling the apostolic injunction and making an attractive advertisement of true Christianity.

Of course, we Europeans were deluged with friendly tokens when we visited his village. What attracted us greatly to him was his unvarying courtesy. No gentleman could be more gallant to the European lady than he. He resented angrily any selfish or thoughtless act which might hurt her, and always made her mere wish the first consideration. Again and again my wife had cause to rejoice in his solicitude for her comfort and her health. Through a severe fever, when she was alone and some distance from home, he nursed her with the sleepless tenderness of a woman, and when some natives had thoughtlessly caused her pain in her sickness they trembled before his tongue as he lashed them for their rudeness.

Once when I was far from well and coming near the time when furlough should be taken, I sat with my elders arranging for certain strenuous meetings which I wished to hold, a series of sacramental gatherings in certain districts, a school for teachers at such and such a date, and so on. But I was annoyed to find Daniel blocking one proposal after another. This gathering could not be held because of some local circumstance : this school would clash with some other duties of the teachers ; and, in the end, only a most attenuated programme was agreed to. It distressed me to think that Daniel was not as keen on getting things done as he used to be.

But that evening I had the key to the subtle diplomacy of my friend when my wife told me that he had been talking to her about my programme,

His Character

had declared that I was ill and was unfit for the work
I wanted to do. So he had diplomatically urged
what difficulties and objections he could find so as
to decrease the volume of work I should be allowed
to undertake.

I thought then it was a delicate and kindly thing
he had done, especially when he knew that he was
causing me to doubt the intensity of his own desire
to push on our service.

With our magistrate, Mr. McDonald, he struck up
a great friendship. Frequently he called on him
when he was near, and sat with him, talking about
his plans for the people. He fearlessly spoke of the
civil evils that were hindering progress, and responded
eagerly to suggestions the magistrate made. It was
his " old-world courtesy," Mr. McDonald afterwards
said, that attracted him to Daniel.

One result of the magistrate's confidence in him
was that he obtained a licence to carry a rifle. Fear
of what might be done with guns led the Government
to confiscate all the old " Tower " muzzle-loading
guns in the tribe, and to limit severely the number of
natives who might own rifles.

But Daniel's work led him constantly through
long stretches of wood and bush-land where wild
beasts of prey roamed, and sometimes into the valleys
and open hills where game abounded. For him a
rifle would be of great value, and his loyalty was
never questioned. He was a careful and accurate
shot. Once or twice I have hunted with him and
seen his craft and patience. He never fired to wound.
His skill in stalking was the result of long years'
training, and he always manœuvred his approach so
that it was almost impossible for him to miss his
quarry. I have seen his eager pursuit of a wounded

His Character

eland, keener and more persistent than that of the finest hound, and he did not stop until he was standing triumphantly over the dead antelope.

One day he and his brother had the good fortune to kill a lioness near his own home and to find four or five little cubs in its den. Three of the cubs were brought to the friendly magistrate and presented to him. For weeks after they played about his verandah and wandered over the golf course and down to the river. But as they grew up they became a cause of terror to the folk who visited the Boma. One day a string of women was going to the river, each carrying her water-pot and gliding along with the graceful carriage that seems natural to all African women. One happening to look behind, saw the young lions creeping after them, their bellies close to the ground as if they were following game. With a yell of terror the women fled, their broken pots strewing the path, while the cubs raced after them with all the joy of young hunters. Another day the little rascals spied the donkey feeding and came up to play with or to attack him. The donkey raised its wise head from the grass and stared at them solemnly, then it stretched its neck and trumpeted forth such a bray that the cubs took to their heels and did not rest until they were safely hiding in their kennel on the verandah.

But their activities were becoming too disconcerting, and soon the magistrate had reluctantly to part with them.

Chapter XXVI

HIS DEATH

WHEN the Great War broke out Nyasaland was immediately drawn into the maelstrom. The Germans attacked at Karonga, one of our stations at the north end of Lake Nyasa, and once more fighting began in this cock-pit of Central Africa. Daniel had been there before with the *impis*, which had left black ruin behind them. For years the fate of Central Africa was at stake while a long fight between the Arab slavers and a little band of Europeans was continued there until it ended in the complete rout of the Arabs. Again the guns were firing, and a small force of British colonial volunteers was camped in the mission grounds and within the trading stations.

Native carriers were needed to bring up provisions and ammunition for the white and black soldiers who held the lines, and the call for volunteers was sent out from the Bomas. Among the first to offer was Daniel. He pressed his services on the magistrate and would not be denied. But Mr. McDonald knew him well, and was fully aware that a man nearly fifty years of age, with a delicate frame, would not stand the hardships of campaigning. Besides, he was sure that Daniel's influence among his own people was so great that he must be kept among them. So he wisely refused to allow him to go to the front.

There was nothing for it but to accept this decision, and during the next months he applied himself with all his might, not only to his primary work of evangelisation, but also to rousing his people to give what loyal service they could in sending forward volunteer carriers and in providing from their gardens food-stuffs for the troops.

One day in session we discussed the approaching induction of Andrew and Daniel. The stated period of probation was finished, but the upset of the war delayed the steps the Presbytery should take before the solemn act of ordination. In his impatience Daniel interposed with one remark. " Let us be ordained before we die ! " he cried. But when at last the great day did come, Andrew stood alone before the vast congregation, for his lifelong colleague had been called to higher service.

Eagerly Daniel followed the news of the war, and his ardent military spirit chafed under its continued indecisiveness. The whole strategy of the East African campaign was a mystery to him. It was so unlike the rapid methods of his old fighting days. When carriers returned from their terms of service he listened with avidity to all the stories they had to tell of the wonderful instruments of warfare they had seen in use.

No doubt entered his mind that it would be an untold calamity did Germany ever get possession of the Red Land. For now clearer and more authentic news was coming through of the massacre on the other side of Lake Nyasa of Abangoni who had fallen under the heavy hand of Germany.

His Death

But he was wild with indignation, too, at the sufferings of his own tribesmen who had gone to the front as carriers. He was always ready to grant that it was " no picnic," and that human feelings had to be suppressed and the carriers driven that supplies might be in time. But he heard too many stories from the men who returned to allow him to believe that they were always considerately treated.

In 1917 the sufferings of our natives were great indeed. Medical and ordinary human care seem to have been denied them, and strings of poor creatures, worn out with dysentery, began to struggle home. Many died by the path. Others found their way to our hospital only to die there, and others crept home to their villages to live in chronic pain and discomfort till death took them. Meanwhile the sick were infecting the whole land. Streams and village outskirts were polluted, and the population was stricken with dysentery.

Knowing the feeble frame of our friend Daniel, and that already he had been seriously ill too often, and that intestinal and lung trouble were his weak points, it was with some alarm that we heard that he and his whole family were lying ill with dysentery at his home forty miles away from us. They had been carried out, after the native fashion, to a temporary house in the bush to try whether a change of location would benefit them.

My wife sent a quantity of medicine to him with careful instructions. But the news of his illness had come to us after many days, and when our messenger arrived at the village he found that Yobe, Daniel's brother, had carried him off to Kasungu, thirty miles farther south, to put him under the care of Dr. Prentice, in whom he had great confidence. They

His Death

arrived to find that Dr. Prentice had been called up for war service and there was no white man on the station. However, a Government veterinary surgeon happened to be in the neighbourhood, and when he heard of Daniel's plight he did what he could to relieve him. But the dysentery was now too far advanced, and all his kindness and skill could do little to arrest the disease.

Yobe then decided to take him back seventy miles to Loudon and put him under the care of my wife. But Daniel knew he was dying, and in the depression of his sickness he would not allow any more to be done for him. Yobe, however, took matters into his own hands and sent messengers on ahead to tell us that he was bringing his brother to hospital. We sent off in all haste a comfortable rickshaw to make the journey easier and swifter for the patient. But when our men met Daniel's bearers they found him too weak to sit up, and they helped to carry him in the hammock in which he was slowly being borne north. One evening we heard they were approaching and we went out to meet them.

When they carried him in I did not recognise my old friend, so thin and wasted was he. His great eyes looked at me solemnly out of his worn skeleton, with a pathos so deep and silent that I had to turn away. But when my wife came to him his old courtesy triumphed again, and he gave her a gentle smile of recognition.

We laid him in bed in a little house near the hospital, and there his wife and brother sat with him untiringly watching every movement.

Next day he rallied slightly, but in the afternoon my wife saw that death was drawing near. She had been kneeling by his bedside for a long time, watching

His Death

each movement and breath, and was unable to restrain her tears while she ministered to the dear man. Then he spoke in a little whisper, begging her to go and lie down for a little and rest herself. In spite of his weakness the gentleman had appeared again.

That evening the end came. When Daniel knew that death was near he began to give broken directions about the guardianship of his children and the distribution of his property. A heathen relative asked him what was to be done with the child who had killed his daughter. Now was the characteristic opportunity of a native death-bed to leave an inheritance of rancour and violence. I have seen these last testimonies, with their charges of witchcraft and the reopening of old sores, lead to bloodshed and never-ending feuds. But Daniel's reply was a feeble effort to sing " Nearer my God to Thee." I did not recognise the song of his panting breath, but his brother and wife did, and they sang the first verse together, but could go no farther for tears.

Then Daniel sank into a quiet sleep. As he slept we sang together a beautiful native hymn about " Christ, our Life," and no voice was clearer in the singing than his wife's, in whose lap Daniel was sleeping.

While he slept he passed from us into the glory of the Father.

Next morning his body was carried back to his own village, and all through the long journey the people turned out in weeping crowds to honour his remains.

In Christian faith, with prayer and song, he was buried by the cattle kraal within his own village, his brother Yobe leading the service. Shortly afterwards the elders decided to erect a memorial to him in the form of choir pews in the Loudon church, with

His Death

a simple brass plate to bear his name. All over the scattered Church the people gave their little gifts in memory of a man who had served them for nearly thirty years.

When the story of his peaceful triumphant crossing was told, by his death he preached his greatest sermon.